Matisse, Picasso, Miró
As I Knew Them

Matisse, Picasso, Miró
As I Knew Them

Rosamond Bernier (signature)

Rosamond Bernier

FOREWORD BY JOHN RUSSELL

ALFRED A. KNOPF   NEW YORK   1991

THIS IS A BORZOI BOOK
PUBLISHED BY ALFRED A. KNOPF, INC.

LIBRARY OF CONGRESS CATALOGING-IN-PUBLICATION DATA

Bernier, Rosamond.
    Matisse, Picasso, Miró as I knew them / Rosamond Bernier ; foreword by John Russell. — 1st ed.
        p.   cm.
    ISBN 0-394-58670-0
    1. Matisse, Henri, 1869–1954. 2. Miró, Joan, 1893–1983. 3. Picasso, Pablo, 1881–1973. 4. Artists—France—Biography. 5. Art, French. 6. Art, Modern—20th century—France. 7. Bernier, Rosamond—Friends and associates. I. Title.
    N6848.B38   1991
    709'.2'244—dc20
    [B]   90-26475   CIP

Manufactured in the United States of America
First Edition

For DJ
Mentor, companion, delight

Contents

Foreword

We are sent on earth to bear witness. If we fail in that, posterity will lay a curse on us. But if we do our duty, we may enjoy the kind of auxiliary immortality that attaches to Amaury-Duval in the context of Ingres, to Antonin Proust in the context of Edouard Manet, to Daniel Halévy in the context of Edgar Degas, and to Emile Bernard in the context of Paul Cézanne. These men were around irreplaceable human beings on a day-to-day basis. They remembered how it was. Before it was too late, they wrote it down. We bless them for it.

The practice has not gone out of style. We bless the photographer Brassaï for his notes on Picasso, the poet Marina Tsvetaeva for her notes on Natalia Goncharova, the novelist and playwright Jean Genet for his essay on Alberto Giacometti, the composer John Cage for what he had to say about the young Jasper Johns, and the critic David Sylvester for his conversations with Francis Bacon.

Common to all of them is the element of immediacy. This person was around. That person had access. Opportunities resulted. They did not go to waste. Those who bear witness at such times offer themselves to us as panes of clear glass through which we see the irreplaceable human beings in question in ways that would otherwise be withheld from us.

It is as just such a pane of clear glass that Rosamond Bernier presents herself to us in her reminiscences of Henri Matisse, Pablo Picasso, and Joan Miró. She tells us when she was with them, and why, and what came of it. Where possible, she edits herself out. If Matisse, Picasso, and Miró talked to her, one after the other, as they might not—at that moment—have talked to anyone else, it is for us to say so. She will never point it out.

Many American readers will know by now that on the lecture platform Rosamond Bernier is one of the best speakers to be encountered anywhere, at any time and on any subject. This was never among her ambitions. Some thirty-five years ago, when she first became a prized friend of mine, nothing was further from her mind than to get up and talk in public.

She had never done it, couldn't do it, wouldn't do it. She wouldn't write, either. She did not believe that she or her experiences were anything unusual. In Paris, where she lived for twenty years, she knew all the best artists in town. But, unlike many expatriates, she did not boast about it. The heyday of hype was not yet upon us. Even Braque had his number in the telephone book. She lived (and at that time would have died) for the magazine *L 'Œil*, which she had founded with her then husband in 1955 and edited until 1969. In no other context would she have made her friendships known.

She knew about living art and living artists, but there was a wide range of earlier art as to which she had both a daylong curiosity and a panoramic and quasi-total recall. She was much around architects and could keep up with the brightest among them. She also knew about collectors. Mazarin in the seventeenth century and Mariette in the eighteenth were as alive for her as Paul Mellon in the twentieth. Mazarin and Mariette are not around to be interviewed, and Mr. Mellon is reticence personified, but when Rosamond Bernier made a film about him for CBS she persuaded him to crack an enormous smile at the memory of having once won the Epsom Derby.

Nowhere in Europe was far away, during her twenty years in Paris, and wherever there was something to see, she went and saw it. Collectors and curators in country after country listened for her light, impetuous footfall and could never hear it too often. Then as now, she had a finely developed comic sense, a gift for extended but never tedious anecdote, and a genius—no other word will do—for human contact. People would do things for her that they would do for no one else. In its glory years *L 'Œil* was irradiated by these qualities, and in one context after another the magazine had both a lightness of touch and a pioneering quality that has been much imitated but never equaled.

France had had glorious art publications like *Verve* and *Minotaure* that quite rightly cost the earth. It had had attractive periodicals that were tied, more or less blatantly, to owners and advertisers. It had had pseudo-newspapers that listed every this and every that, with journeyman texts to match.

But *L'Œil* was something quite different—a treasure box of striking and unexpected images that stood for nothing but an individual taste. Though on top of the news, it was not dictated by it. It attracted very good and often unexpected writers—French, English, American. It looked both seductive and serious, and although it was printed in Switzerland and overseen with exemplary care, it was remarkably cheap.

Many readers still cherish their vintage copies of *L'Œil*, though the magazine long ago changed hands. They also cherish the books that came out under the name Editions de l'Œil—among them the first reissue of the collage novel *La Femme 100 Têtes*, by Max Ernst, and Mary McCarthy's *Venice Observed*, which was commissioned and coaxed along by Rosamond Bernier and now has classic status.

Yet there was also within her a potential for independent, single-handed action that had not yet found an outlet. After she came back to the United States in 1969, that potential was released by her friend Michael Mahoney, Professor of Art History at Trinity College in Hartford, Connecticut. It was his idea, first mooted in 1970, that with her firsthand experience of the masters of living art, her fine-grained editorial skills, and her gift for spontaneous presentation, she should give a course at Trinity on the history of twentieth-century art. She could talk as well as anyone around. Why couldn't she teach?

"A course? *Lectures?*" she said, unfeignedly aghast. "How many lectures?" "Fourteen," said Professor Mahoney. "And when do I begin?" "In a month," he said. Anyone else would have freaked out, but in her light-boned and apparently insubstantial frame there was the will to take fate by the throat and shake it. On the appointed day she stood up straight and began.

Leonard Bernstein said of her sometime later on that she had "the gift of instant communication to a degree which I have rarely encountered." As it was in life, so it was in the classroom. In no time at all, as it now seems, that classroom opened up and out, as in a transformation scene in a Renaissance masque. Her white magic worked as well in the Naval War College in Newport, Rhode Island, as in the Grand Palais in Paris (where she spoke in French) and at the World Business Congress in Istanbul.

Above all at the Metropolitan Museum of Art in New York, but no less as a volunteer in Boys Harbor—a not-for-profit agency that reaches out to young people from Harlem between the ages of ten and twelve—she persuaded her audiences that there need be no limits to what would interest and amuse them. Speaking without notes and with hardly a word dropped or searched for, she set her listeners free to be themselves. "That was the best time!" they said as they went home.

Such was her success with audiences of every kind that she could have coasted along with just one or two lectures and a minimal amount of revising and re-rehearsing. But she disdained to do so, preferring to work long days for several months every year on new lectures.

If they were given only once, as was the case with the Yaseen lecture of 1981 at the Metropolitan Museum, on the sculptures of Matisse, she nonetheless gave them her very best shot. If they had a specialized air, as was the case with "Word and Image: Stéphane Mallarmé and Painting," or "Art and the Book," or "The Treasures of Liechtenstein," she lowered her standards not at all but went straight ahead, knowing full well that nobody would walk out. (And nobody did, by the way.)

Over the years, one publisher after another called to ask if she would not publish her lectures in book form. After videotapes of them were shown (more than once) on public television, these inquiries were redoubled. If she always demurred, it was because she knew that what impresses on the podium or at the dinner table can drop dead on the page. Besides, she genuinely could not imagine that anyone would want to buy such a book.

But eventually she was persuaded that her lectures on Matisse, Picasso, and Miró could be reedited and reshaped in the form of a triptych that would read as a book, rather than as a transcript of the spoken word. It is this book that follows this foreword, and I for one am happy to see it.

John Russell

Acknowledgments

S. I. Newhouse, Jr., thought up the idea for this book in the first place and persuaded me that it should be written.

My husband, John Russell, persuaded me that it *could* be written. My hand is in his on every page.

Susan Ralston and Peter Andersen, my editor and designer, respectively, clarified a daunting mass of material with Voltairean precision and an enthusiasm that matched my own. My thanks to Ellen McNeilly, also of Knopf, who taught me about cyan and many other things. I am particularly happy with the stylish book jacket designed by Carol Devine Carson.

My serene assistant, Virginia Rutledge, kept chaos at bay with unflinching efficiency and never-failing grace.

This material might never have appeared in its present form if portions of it had not been originally recorded for videocassette thanks to the sponsorship of the Dillon Fund and the urging of Mrs. Douglas Dillon. I will always be grateful.

I should like to think that this book would have pleased two almost lifelong friends of mine, Pierre Matisse and Roland Penrose, neither of whom is here to read it. They were ever-generous in sharing with me their involvement with the great masters of our century.

Matisse, Picasso, Miró
As I Knew Them

Painter in the Olive Grove, 1923–24. Oil
on canvas, 23 ¾ x 28 ⅞ " (60.3 x 73.4
cm). Baltimore Museum of Art; Cone
Collection, formed by Dr. Claribel
Cone and Miss Etta Cone of Baltimore,
Maryland.

CHAPTER I

Matisse at First Hand

Villa Le Rêve. Photo: Hélène Adant/Rapho.

My first summer in France, as a young writer with her first job—it was in 1947—I was visiting Pablo Picasso near Antibes. A friend offered to arrange an introduction to Henri Matisse. This was an enormously exciting prospect. I of course admired the great man hugely.

Normally, Matisse lived in Cimiez, a suburb above Nice. But in March 1943, when Allied landings were believed to be imminent, Cimiez was thought to be too exposed. So Matisse moved inland and up to the hilltop village of Vence, where he rented a villa.

How to get there? There was no public transport, and there were few cars available at this time, soon after the war, but I finally rounded up an extremely ancient taxi belonging to an even more ancient driver, and he agreed to take me to Vence.

My appointment with Matisse was at noon. We set out in good time but soon, to my dismay, it became clear that we were hopelessly lost. My driver admitted he wasn't from the region, he just happened to be spending holidays there with his cab; there were no signposts (they'd been removed during the war). We looped and turned through pleated hillsides terraced into vineyards, past shiny greenhouses crammed with carnations. (This is the carnation-growing center of France.) What might have looked—and did look—beautiful to me on other occasions now looked like Dante's Inferno, as I panted and panicked and saw the hour growing later and later.

What made it almost worse was that everything I saw through the window reminded me of Matisse. Here I was, in the country he had made his own, and yet I despaired of ever finding him.

It was one o'clock before we got to Vence, and then we had to find the house itself. To keep a distinguished old gentleman waiting is bad enough—but to keep a Frenchman from his lunch!

We finally found the house on the outskirts of the town—a very ordinary ocher box of a villa called Le Rêve (The Dream). But I was to find out later that Matisse had indeed transformed it into a dream. Heart beating, I walked up the little path and rang the doorbell.

The door was opened by what appeared to me then to be a very formidable female. Her handsome blue eyes and strong features were familiar to me: she was Madame Lydia Delektorskaya, who for years had been Matisse's model, assistant, nurse, and housekeeper. I recognized her immediately; I recognized just as clearly that she was furious, and not at all the relaxed voluptuous beauty, often undressed, whom I remembered from his paintings and drawings of her from the thirties.

"You're late," she said accusingly. I was ready to flee. Then a stocky figure loomed in the hallway, wearing an open-necked white shirt and dark blue trousers, glowering.

It was Matisse himself. "You're late," he echoed Madame Lydia. I hoped that the earth would open up and swallow me. But he cut through my stammered apologies: "Well, as long as you're here, you might as well come in for a moment."

We sat down. I was far too nervous even to notice what was around me. There was Henri Matisse facing me—neatly trimmed white beard, gold-rimmed specs—looking like a prosperous banker on holiday. What he was saying, after a few brief preliminaries, only made everything worse.

"Madame," he said—he was to call me "Madame" until the end of his days, although I was young at the time and he was to show me many

Reclining Nude on a Violet Background,
1936. Oil on canvas.
Private collection.

Matisse drawing *La Martiniquaise*.
Photo: Hélène Adant/Rapho.

kindnesses—"before we go any further, allow me to point out that you owe me thirty-eight dollars."

I was dumbfounded: I had never seen him before, nor had I had any dealings with him.

"I believe you write for *Vogue* magazine?" he continued. I admitted that I did.

"Well, *Vogue* published a work of mine before the war and never paid me the rights. Thirty-eight dollars, please."

I explained that I had just come from the beach and had no dollars with me.

"A check will do," said Matisse.

I had to explain that I didn't have a checkbook in my little beach basket.

"*I* have one," he said, getting up. He came back into the room with his checkbook.

I was so new in France that I didn't even know how to write out a check in French—and so it was under the dictation of one of the masters

Matisse in his Vence garden. Photo: Hélène Adant/Rapho.

of the twentieth century that I wrote for the benefit of my New York bank that I owed him thirty-eight dollars. This worried me from every point of view. For one thing, this was my first job and I was none too sure that I *had* thirty-eight dollars in my account.

I noticed that he was watching my pen—it was a new-model Parker, not yet known in France. On an impulse I said, "Won't you try it?" and handed it to him. He liked the way it would draw a line flowingly to the left or right. "Please keep it," I urged him.

Without a change of expression, looking as severe as ever, he said, "*Un instant, s'il vous plaît,*" and left the room. He came back, smiling this time, holding out something to me. It was his own pen. "I'll keep yours on condition you keep mine," he said.

Then I knew the ice was broken. I began to breathe at a more normal rate. And while Matisse had been out of the room, Madame Lydia had come over and said kindly, "Don't worry. Monsieur Matisse likes you. I can tell. You will be able to come back."

I felt vastly relieved but knew I shouldn't push my luck. I started for the door. Matisse followed me.

"The best bistro in the region is just a quarter of an hour away," he said, "and the best dish they make is a *loup flambé au fenouil*"—Mediterranean sea bass cooked over fennel. "It takes them a while to prepare it— but I have telephoned and reserved your table, and I've ordered the *loup* for you so you won't have to wait."

This little story tells us quite a lot about Henri Matisse. As a pragmatist (don't forget he came from hard-headed peasant stock from the north of France), he never lost sight of the practical details of life—the thirty-eight dollars. But as a sensualist he never lost sight of this world's pleasures and delights.

On the way to lunch—which, incidentally, was all that he said it would be—I thought over my visit to Matisse. Although he was by then nearly eighty years old and not at all well, he had radiated an extraordinary serenity. I had no trouble believing that this was indeed the man who had painted picture after picture that brought the Golden Age to life.

The Golden Age is usually situated way back in time and steeped in mythology. Titian, Giorgione, and Giovanni Bellini were some of the Italian old masters who had evoked it to perfection. Modern times played no part in it. But for Henri Matisse, the Golden Age was strictly of his own day and his own invention. It had come to him in Nice, the big city by the sea that was only a few miles from Vence.

He had arrived in Nice in his late forties, a man from the north who

Matisse sketching in his Vence garden.
Photo: Hélène Adant/Rapho.

ABOVE:
Festival of Flowers, 1921. Oil on canvas,
28½ x 39" (72.5 x 99 cm). Private
collection, Zurich.

OPPOSITE:
The Bay of Nice, 1918. Oil on canvas,
35⅜ x 28" (90 x 71 cm). Private
collection.

Woman Sitting on a Balcony with Violet Stockings and a Green Parasol, 1919. Oil on canvas, 16½ x 13" (42 x 33 cm). Collection Annick and Pierre Berès, Paris.

could not get over his pleasure, his excitement, and his good fortune at being an honorary southerner. In Nice he had found a new landscape, a new light, a new warmth, a new life. The view from his window made him giddy, in more senses than one, and as for the annual parade, the Festival of Flowers, he felt as if it had been run up expressly to make him feel at home.

Matisse had first glimpsed the Golden Age in 1917, when he asked Laurette, his favorite model, to look her very best while lying down.

There were no fauns or centaurs in his Golden Age, no satyrs, no gods or goddesses. Life was lived out in hotels and apartments and balconies overlooking a southern sea. Pretty women lolled around doing nothing much of anything. Nobody was old or ugly, unhappy or sick. Nobody wore couture clothes, but they didn't look like frumps, either. If they felt like wearing violet stockings and big black shoes with bows on them, they went ahead and did it. Sometimes they dressed up, but mostly they dressed down. Other people did the housework. The cut flowers never died, there were always delicious things to eat, and it never seemed to rain.

There was never a man in sight, though sometimes Matisse himself could be glimpsed, painting away in his pajamas. Of human conflict, real or imagined, there was no trace. The pictures looked as if they had been painted without effort and could give no one any trouble.

Even if you knew some art history you had to remind yourself that this was the same man whose *Blue Nude* (page 12) had been burned in effigy by art students in Chicago when the Armory Show was on view there, in 1913, after its first showing in New York. No one in our century had painted tougher or more challenging pictures than Matisse.

Laurette with a Cup of Coffee, 1917. Oil on canvas, 35 x 57½" (89 x 146 cm). Private collection.

The Painter and His Model, 1919. Oil on canvas, 23 ⅝ x 28 ¾" (60 x 73 cm). Collection Mr. and Mrs. Donald B. Marron, New York.

Still Life (with Pineapple, Compote, Fruits, Vase of Anemones), 1925. Oil on canvas, 31 ⅞ x 39 ⅜" (81 x 100 cm). Philadelphia Museum of Art, Henry P. McIlhenny Collection in Memory of Frances P. McIlhenny.

Blue Nude (Souvenir of Biskra), 1907.
Oil on canvas, 36¼ x 56⅛" (92.1 x
142.5 cm). Baltimore Museum of Art;
Cone Collection, formed by Dr. Claribel Cone and Miss Etta Cone of Baltimore, Maryland.

The Moroccans, 1916. Oil on canvas,
71 ⅜ x 110" (181.3 x 279.4 cm). Collection, The Museum of Modern Art, New
York; Gift of Mr. and Mrs. Samuel A.
Marx.

In 1916, he painted *The Moroccans* (page 13), a picture that still startles by its abrupt schematic way with a group of Moroccans prostrated in prayer. For years, there were people who thought that the bowed heads were king-sized vegetables on offer in a Moroccan market.

All that had changed by the 1920s. But there were severe critics then, and one or two are still around today, who rather deplored the Nice pictures. They found them too easy, too seductive, too much of an apology for a leisured class, and too remote from what is now called "the real world." "Appeasing the bourgeoisie," they said. Matisse the avant-garde master had sold out and sold up, in their view, and settled for painting pretty pictures for pretty people.

That point of view did not survive a visit to the Matisse exhibition "The Early Years in Nice: 1916–1930," which opened in 1986 at the

Odalisque in Red Trousers, 1922. Oil on canvas, 26⅜ x 33⅛" (67 x 84 cm). Musée National d'Art Moderne, Centre Georges Pompidou, Paris.

National Gallery of Art in Washington, D.C. It is of course true that there is a contrast between the bare-bones quality and the gaunt, condemned-cell atmosphere of the great *Studio, Quai Saint-Michel*, which was done in Paris in 1916, and the relaxed, easygoing look of *The Moorish Screen*, which was done only a few years later in Nice. The one speaks for the painting as an affair of weight and moment. The other speaks for the studio as a subdepartment of paradise.

But the lesson of the National Gallery show was that Matisse during his early years in Nice was an immensely more complicated and ambitious painter than had ever been realized before. For size of output, level of quality, and variety of ambition, this was a period of sustained achievement such as has rarely been rivaled in our century.

On one level, many of these paintings have a sharpness of social observation that is quite exceptional. Matisse monitored how women dressed, how they did their hair, and how they made up their eyebrows and lips. He was a master of the body language that Frenchwomen of his day adopted in trivial social situations. When it came to painting women's hats he had no equal.

TOP:
Woman in a Blue Hat, 1922. Oil on canvas, 28 ¾ x 23 ½" (73 x 59.7 cm). Collection Arnold A. Saltzman and family.

BOTTOM:
Marguerite in a Plaid Coat, 1918. Oil on canvas, 37 ⅜ x 29 ½" (95 x 75 cm). Collection Mr. A. Alfred Taubman.

Those hats were really portraits. Matisse knew all about women's hats. His wife had worked as a milliner in the early days to help support the family. Matisse himself had pinned together an extraordinary plumed hat that was recorded in a number of paintings. Then when life was easier, he sent his wife and daughter, Marguerite, to a fashionable modiste named Jeanne on the rue Royale.

Not only was Matisse extremely elegant in his own person—real linen trousers, loose summer jackets of raw silk—but he had a lively interest in fashion. A friend of the family was Germaine Bongard, sister of Paul Poiret, and a couturière herself. Matisse saw to it that his wife and daughter dressed at Madame Bongard's. He also helped to choose the models and supervised the fittings.

When I visited Matisse, I always made a point of trying to choose something to wear that would amuse him. I was rewarded. "Go and stand by the white door so that I can look at you," he would say, or, "What have you done for color today?"

At one time I had a big orange coat by Balenciaga. "Wear a yellow scarf with it," he advised. I did.

But it was not Matisse's object to contribute to the human comedy as Bonnard or Vuillard had done. He wanted to downplay and almost annihilate the human presence by giving it only equal time—and sometimes not even that—with every other element in the painting. The human figure was there to catch light, to mark a space, and to observe a total neutrality. Above all, it was not to have a vibration with which we can identify.

The paintings, not the person, vibrated. And the paint, not the piano, made music.

If it sounds like a tough program, that's exactly what it was. Matisse made wonderful still lifes in Nice, and enormous flower pieces that gave the genre a new dimension. He worked all day, every day, only taking time off to clock up an impressive number of sorties in a single scull. But it was in painting, above all, that he pushed himself as far as he could go.

After that first visit, and the affair of the check and the pen, Matisse and I became friends, and we remained so until his death. Informal conversation and jocular remarks were not his style. But when I married, he sent an engraved visiting card (with a hyphen between "Henri" and "Matisse," as he often signed himself), wishing me "complete and unlimited happiness."

Pianist and Checker Players, 1924. Oil
on canvas, 29⅛ x 36⅜" (74 x 92.1 cm).
National Gallery of Art, Washington,
D.C.; Collection of Mr. and Mrs. Paul
Mellon.

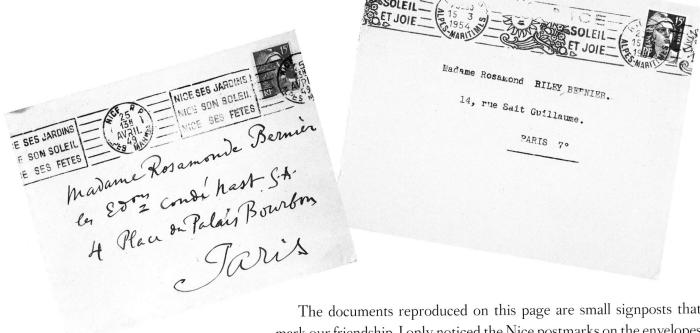

The documents reproduced on this page are small signposts that mark our friendship. I only noticed the Nice postmarks on the envelopes many years after I received them. The earlier one, dated 1949, is stamped with Nice's happy boast: "Nice—its gardens, its sunshine, its *fêtes*." Matisse might have written that himself. The other one, sent the year Matisse died, 1954, is stamped repeatedly "*Soleil et Joie*"—"Sunshine and Joy." This touched me very much because that is just what his paintings suggest when we first see them. As Picasso used to say, "Matisse carries a sun with a thousand rays in his stomach."

Matisse sketched a quizzical little self-portrait for me in 1948. He seemed to me so measured, so balanced, so controlled—and yet, he said, he had spent his entire life working to bring order to a naturally chaotic nature.

I had enjoyed the earlier self-portrait drawings, with their floppy, hesitant look, but when I next went to see Matisse there was nothing either floppy or hesitant about what he had to show me. It was the work of someone who was at the top of his form, and in quite a new way.

What he had to show me, to begin with, was the great series of interiors he had painted in 1947–48. He explained to me that he had had a grave operation in 1941 and a long convalescence. During that time he could work only in bed, so painting was almost out of the question. He drew a great deal, and he made some of the book illustrations that can be seen on pages 37, 38, and 39.

Now, although not, unfortunately, for long, he was able to stand and paint again, and this master of color said, "I feel all the curiosity of a traveler in a foreign land. I have never gone forward so totally in the expression of color."

This series shows his Vence living room, which also served as an improvised studio. Most of the paintings follow a theme long dear to him: the relationship between inside space and outside space—an interior, a window, and what can be seen beyond a window. The idea of the window as a transparency that could let in either the distant horizon or nearby garden trees, and yet be a barrier, had fascinated Matisse all his life.

Among the new paintings was the *Red Interior* in which the open-window theme was treated with the kind of daring that sometimes comes to a great old man in the plenitude of his powers. The overrunning pattern of black zigzag lines on red covered the walls, the floor, and the

Red Interior, Still Life on a Blue Table, 1947. Oil on canvas, 45 ⅝ x 35" (116 x 89 cm). Kunstsammlung Nordrhein-Westfalen, Düsseldorf.

The Pineapple, 1948. Oil on canvas,
45 ¾ x 35" (116.2 x 88.9 cm). Alex
Hillman Family Foundation.

Large Red Interior, 1948. Oil on canvas,
57½ x 38⅛" (146 x 97 cm). Musée
National d'Art Moderne, Centre
Georges Pompidou, Paris.

terrace outside. Flower beds and palm trees in blossom were brought up
flat against the picture plane. Matisse took every possible liberty, and yet
the picture reads as easily as if it had been painted in strict perspective.

As for the 1948 *Large Red Interior*, it is triumphantly, overwhelmingly
red. There is no attempt to suggest depth: the artist has taken the same
intense color and carried it from the foreground, along the floor, and up
the back wall, with no diminution in value. Balancing this brilliance are
two of Matisse's own works—a large China-ink drawing and a study of a
pineapple. A prim Dutch chair separates the curvy-legged outlines of
two tables. The yellow shapes up front are animal skin rugs.

The Pineapple is the only one of the series that concentrates on a single object. The pineapple itself, a delicate gray, nestles in the mountain-

LEFT:
The Silence Living in Houses, 1947. Oil on canvas, 28 x 19⅝" (61 x 50 cm). Private collection.

RIGHT:
Window of Villa Le Rêve, 1946. Photo: Hélène Adant/Rapho.

ous peaks of its wrapping paper, while colors eddy around it in almost abstract swirls.

At this time, 1948, Matisse made some monumental brush-and-ink drawings of themes he had treated before in oil. These powerful drawings, Matisse said, had the same intensity for him as the richly colored paintings.

It also interested him to simplify the great subjects that had always preoccupied him—the symphonic still life and the open window—in terms of the rich and sonorous blacks that he discovered, in his graphic works, late in life.

There were a number of variations on the inside-outside theme. *The Silence Living in Houses* included the shadowy presence of two girls hovering in the left-hand corner. Color once again is used not to describe the scene, but to express Matisse's feelings. It is clear from the view outside the window that the Midi sun is blazing, but a cool, quiet interior is suggested by nocturnal walls. *Interior with Black Fern* is alive with pattern, with a staccato speckled floor, dotted vase, and striped chair-back dominated by the black plant that balances the palm fronds seen through the window.

A palm tree seen through a window was a recurring motif in Matisse's work. It appears in some of those glorious, resonant brush-and-ink drawings, and also in a photograph taken from his living room window.

Photographs show us how faithful Matisse always was to the inner truth of a given scene, even if he sometimes seemed to blast off into a distilled and purified version of what was on the other side of the window. One such photograph echoes the olive trees beyond the window in *The Silence: Living in Houses.*

The Egyptian Curtain (page 24), an extraordinary picture in the Phillips Collection in Washington, D.C., is the culmination of the inside-outside series. Matisse has the nerve to hold a curtain with an impossibly blatant pattern right up next to our eyes, and yet balance it by the explo-

LEFT:
Dahlias and Pomegranates, 1947. Brush and ink on white paper, 30 x 22¼" (76.2 x 56.5 cm). Collection, The Museum of Modern Art, New York. Abby Aldrich Rockefeller Fund.

RIGHT:
Interior with Black Fern, 1948. Oil on canvas, 45 ¾ x 35" (116.2 x 88.9 cm). Private collection, Switzerland.

OVERLEAF, LEFT:
The Egyptian Curtain, 1948. Oil on canvas, 45 ¾ x 35" (116.2 x 88.9 cm). Phillips Collection, Washington, D.C.

OVERLEAF, RIGHT:
Pablo Picasso, *The Artist's Studio*, 1955. Oil on canvas, 31 ⅞ x 25 ⅝" (81 x 65 cm). Present location unknown.

Pablo Picasso, sketch of a bearded painter, inscribed on the back of the sheet, from a notebook of 1971.

sion of palm fronds "whizzing like rockets" outside the window, as Alfred H. Barr, Jr., described it in his pioneering but still indispensable work, *Matisse: His Art and His Public*. The pink table and bowl of pomegranates provide an oasis of calm between the two areas of dissonance.

The same theme was treated by another great painter living in the south of France at the same time, Pablo Picasso. In the 1950s, Picasso bought a big villa above Cannes, called La Californie, and he used to work in its Art Nouveau living room. In his version (page 25), a strong linear rhythm, not color, is what counts. The arabesques of the turn-of-the-century French windows separate the dark interior from the lemon Mediterranean sky, against which incisively drawn palm trees are seen in silhouette.

For anyone who was on calling terms with both of these twentieth-century masters, a certain diplomacy was essential. It was not a good idea to let one know you had just seen—or might be about to see—the other, although they always guessed. Matisse would ask me in an offhand way, "I suppose you have seen Picasso?" and Picasso, jauntily, would ask, "What's Matisse up to these days?"

By the time I knew them, there had been a lifetime of wary, watchful admiration. Matisse was the elder of the two by twelve years. When the very young Picasso arrived in Paris from Barcelona, Matisse was already a married man with a family and a reputation. Matisse's serene progress was to be severely jolted by the cataclysms of Cubism and Picasso's continual artistic convulsions.

Picasso, who had a gift for the lapidary phrase, summed up the differences between himself and Matisse: "North Pole, South Pole." They were as far apart, or so it seemed to me, as it was possible for two men to be. They stood for antithetical extremes. Matisse looked like the epitome of French reason, lucidity, perseverance, and sense of proportion. Picasso was all instinct, all impulse, all headlong passion. Each had what the other had not, and to that extent they complemented one another.

But by Matisse's last year—he died in 1954—all old rivalries were forgotten and devoted admiration took over. Picasso used to be driven to Cimiez (Matisse had moved back to his large studio-apartment there) to see Matisse, and sometimes he took new work along, strapped on top of his car, to show his old friend.

After Matisse died, Picasso said, "I have to paint for both of us now."

Picasso drew everywhere, everyone, all the time, as he breathed. His family told me he could draw before he could talk. He sometimes

Marguerite, 1907. Oil on canvas, 25 ⅝ x
21 ¼" (65 x 54 cm). Musée Picasso,
Paris.

appeared to be quite surprised at the figures that emerged on his sketch
pad. Once when I was with him he was turning over pages of drawings
and came across the figure of a bearded painter. "It looks a bit like
Matisse, don't you think?" he asked. I agreed. Whereupon he wrote on
the back of the sheet, "*Un peu Matisse*"—"a little like Matisse." By then,
1971, Matisse had been dead seventeen years.

After showing me this drawing, Picasso said, "Come and see something," and he took me to his atelier. There were a number of paintings
by Matisse lined up on the floor against the wall. He used to joke: "I am
the world's biggest collector of Matisse"—he owned seven. "More and
more, I feel the need to live with these."

The two artists exchanged pictures on a number of occasions. I
remembered a Picasso landscape of the 1940s over Matisse's living room
fireplace in Vence. Matisse's 1907 portrait of his daughter—she wears a
black band to hide a recent throat operation—came to live with Picasso
shortly after it was painted.

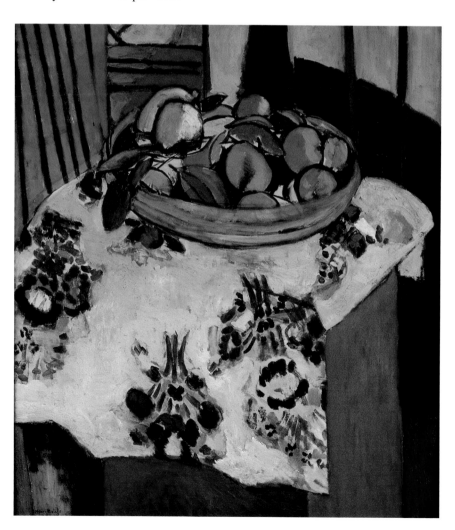

Basket of Oranges, 1913. Oil on canvas,
37 x 32 ⅝" (94 x 83 cm). Musée
Picasso, Paris.

Theme F, Variation 3, 1941. Pen and ink, 20½ x 15 ¾" (52.2 x 30 cm). Musée de Peinture et de Sculpture, Grenoble.

RIGHT:
Theme F, Variation 1, 1941. Charcoal, 15 ¾ x 20½" (30 x 52.2 cm). Musée de Peinture et de Sculpture, Grenoble.

OPPOSITE, TOP:
Study of Fruit and Flowers, Theme, 1942. Charcoal, 16 x 20½" (40.6 x 52 cm). Musée des Beaux-Arts, Bordeaux.

OPPOSITE, BOTTOM:
Study of Fruit and Flowers, Variation 6, 1942. Pencil, 19¼ x 23 ⅝" (49 x 60 cm). Musée des Beaux-Arts, Bordeaux.

But the sumptuous *Basket of Oranges* (page 27), painted by Matisse in Morocco in 1913, was bought by Picasso during World War II. He was immensely proud of it and showed it off to visitors. I was taken to admire it during one of my first visits to Picasso's Paris atelier in the rue des Grands-Augustins. Perhaps in honor of this acquisition, Matisse used to send a crate of oranges to Picasso every New Year's. Picasso was immensely proud of these, too. He would point them out to friends, saying, "These are Matisse's oranges, you know," as if that made them completely different from any oranges ever grown before.

Picasso was also very touched when, after Matisse's death, his family sent over a cabinet full of specially designed drawers that Matisse had made for his drawings. "Isn't that just like Matisse?" Picasso said. "I think of him every day when I look at it."

Matisse had a certain professorial side, and when he felt he had a sympathetic listener he was generous about explaining why he worked in a certain manner. He often talked to me about drawing. (Such a conversation would have been unthinkable with Picasso.)

When he had been bedridden and too ill to paint, during World War II, Matisse drew all the time. His drawings may look like the work of a carefree hedonist, but in reality they were the result of implacably demanding discipline. What appeared to be as spontaneous as the flight of a swallow was endlessly rehearsed and came about through arduous repetition.

In 1941, Matisse wrote to his son Pierre (who for sixty years, until his death in 1989, was a well-known New York art dealer): "For a year now I've been making an enormous effort in drawing. I say effort, but that's not right. What has occurred is a *floraison* [flowering] after fifty years of effort."

Matisse likened the act of drawing to the limbering-up exercises of a dancer or an acrobat. Like an acrobatic feat, it couldn't be modified in midair: it must be successfully executed in the empty white space of a sheet of paper.

At that time, his manner of working was to draw the same subject over and over again, each time on a different sheet—no erasures, no corrections. These scores of drawings zeroed in on the subject, reducing it ever further to its essentials. Usually, the last version eliminates even more details. Shading and modeling disappear and the flowing line alone carries the message.

Sometimes he named a series of drawings as if it were a piece of music—a *Theme and Variations*. There was a suite of seventeen such movements or themes. Some centered around fruit and flowers (page 28), others were figure pieces (page 29). Matisse referred to them in a letter to Pierre in 1945 as "a motion picture of the feelings of an artist."

One time when I went to see Matisse, I noticed a sketch in white chalk on the inside of his living room door. "What's that?" I asked. "I had been working all morning from the model," he explained. "I wanted to know if I really had it in my fingers. So I had myself blindfolded, and I walked to the door and drew."

The chalk sketch was almost as firm as the drawing on paper.

Matisse told me that a few years before, a documentary film had been made of him. In one sequence, he is shown drawing, in slow motion. "Before my pencil even touched the paper," he said, "my hand made a strange journey of its own. I never realized before that I did this. I suddenly felt as if I were shown naked . . . that everyone could see this . . . it made me feel deeply ashamed.

"You must understand," he continued, "this was not hesitation. I was unconsciously establishing the relationship between the subject I was about to draw and the size of my paper. *Je n'avais pas encore commencé à chanter.*" [I had not yet begun to sing.]

"What interests me most is not a still life, or a landscape, but the figure. It is this that allows me to express my almost religious feeling for life," he said. (He was referring to a purely personal sense of religion.) For Matisse, "the figure" almost always meant the body of a woman. The charcoal drawings of the female nude that date from the 1940s have a delectable smoothness of contour. But they also have the firmness of young bodies gripped and held fast.

It is clear from his work, if not always from the face that he presented to the world, that Matisse loved women. In fact he loved them so much that we feel he would have liked to possess them all. In his paintings he could act that out.

In his first years in Nice, he lived in hotel rooms. But as of 1921 he had his own apartment there, and quite soon he made it into a place of fantasy, a twentieth-century harem in which beautiful women lay around awaiting his pleasure.

It helped that Matisse had a passion for the richly patterned universe of Islamic art. He had spent several winters soaking up the Moorish tradition at first hand in Morocco and Andalusia. In Nice, he re-created a little corner of this world in his atelier—a miniature theater set with exotic decor: Moorish screens, Arab carpets, intricately patterned fab-

LEFT:
Nude Study, 1947. Charcoal, 14⅛ x 10½" (36 x 26.5 cm).

RIGHT:
Nude Study, 1947. Charcoal.

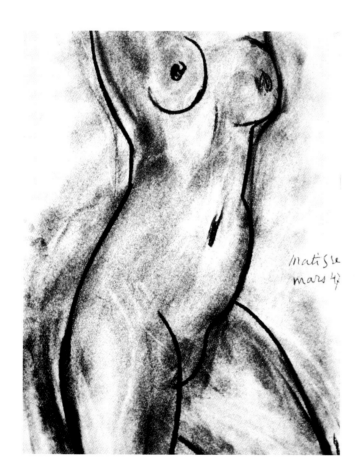
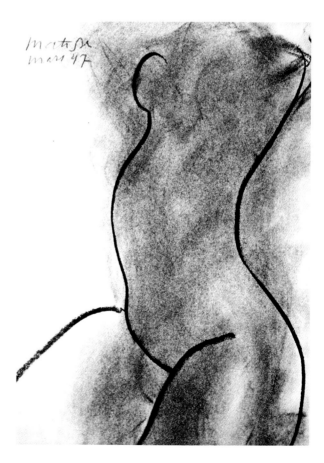

Matisse and his model Henriette Darricarrère, Nice, c. 1928. Photographer
unknown.

OPPOSITE:
*Seated Odalisque, Left Knee Bent, Orna-
mental Background and Checkerboard*,
1928. Oil on canvas, 21⅝ x 14⅞" (55 x
37.8 cm). Baltimore Museum of Art;
Cone Collection, formed by Dr. Claribel Cone and Miss Etta Cone of Baltimore, Maryland.

rics, a North African stool, a brass stove. Against these *souvenirs de
voyage* he posed his models costumed in gauzy pantaloons, transparent
veiling, embroidered jackets. They lounged among cushions and rug-
strewn divans.

For Matisse the south of France was a place where voluptuous women
could loll around all day half undressed and see no reason to change their
ways. And when he came to paint them, he shipped them to an imagined

Odalisque with Green Sash, 1926–27.
Oil on canvas, 20 x 25 ½" (50.8 x 64.8
cm). Baltimore Museum of Art; Cone
Collection, formed by Dr. Claribel
Cone and Miss Etta Cone of Baltimore,
Maryland.

Matisse and the author, 1948. Photo: Clifford Coffin/Condé Nast.

Africa. Nice for him became a station stop on the way to Algiers and Fez and Marrakech, and the personable young women who posed for him at so much an hour became prisoners of his harem.

Matisse managed to make the sun shine steadily for his odalisques. They could take their ease in the thinnest veiling without a shiver. But when he asked me to come to see him in Vence one November day, it was piercingly cold and layers of wool jersey were in order.

He himself was in bed—a recurrence of old troubles—but the visible part of him was arranged with the utmost formality: tie, matching sweater, faultlessly trimmed beard.

He had prepared a marvelous feast for me. He had set out all the books he had illustrated, and he pointed out one example after another to show exactly why and how he had solved certain problems about the "ornamentation," as he called it, of a book. He explained that he saw no difference between building a book and building a painting. It was a question of balancing a light page and a dark page against each other.

Matisse cared about the way the line of a drawing flowed across the page, and he also cared about the look of the written word. Even in a casual note such as the one reproduced on page 36, every mark has its

Letter to the author from Henri
Matisse, 1949.

Le Cygne, 1930–32, from *Poésies* by
Stéphane Mallarmé, published by
Albert Skira, Lausanne, 1932. Etching,
printed in black, page size 13 x 9⅞"
(33 x 25 cm). Collection, The Museum
of Modern Art, New York, Louis E.
Stern Collection.

Matisse sketching a swan in the Bois de
Boulogne. Photo: Pierre Matisse.

chosen place. His signature is as much danced as written, with the three
stalwart bars of the "M" followed by the lilt of the double "s."He loved
words. He loved reading—poetry in particular. He was a natural for mar-
rying images with text.

But he was sixty years old before anyone asked him to illustrate a
book. The first time was in 1930, when the Swiss publisher Albert Skira
invited him to illustrate the poems of Stéphane Mallarmé, a great
favorite of Matisse's. He was delighted.

One of the poems was about a swan. Now, Matisse knew perfectly
well what a swan looked like, but—typical of his thoroughgoing, serious
approach to everything—he went out to the Bois de Boulogne, sat in a
little boat on the lake, and sketched swans from life. As is well known,
swans can be very bad-tempered creatures, and the great artist wasn't
spared their irascibility. One of his models kept swiveling around, hissing alarmingly, as Matisse recorded in one of his sketches.

Matisse made a great number of drawings for the Mallarmé project.

Finally twenty-seven etchings were chosen for the disembodied purity they had achieved, a purity that matches the evanescent quality of Mallarmé's poetry.

During that period in the early 1940s when he had to stay in bed—between 1941 and 1944, roughly—Matisse started what became a great series of illustrated books. He chose mainly poets such as Charles d'Orléans, Ronsard, Baudelaire, Mallarmé—all of whom had celebrated love and the beauty of women.

He talked about two different approaches he had taken in illustrating two different books, pointing at specific examples with a well-manicured finger. For the Mallarmé, he wanted to make an illustration so light that it would leave the page almost as white as before it was printed. In this way the drawn line would not outweigh the airy quality of the text. He decided to use a very fine line, without shading, and to float it over the entire page, without margins. This would give a lightness that would not have been possible if the illustration had been massed in the center.

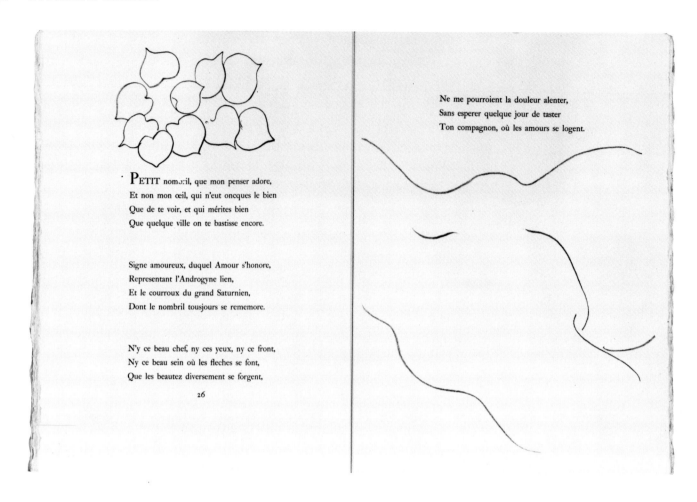

Ne me pourroient la douleur alenter,
Sans esperer quelque jour de taster
Ton compagnon, où les amours se logent.

PETIT nombril, que mon penser adore,
Et non mon œil, qui n'eut oncques le bien
Que de te voir, et qui mérites bien
Que quelque ville on te bastisse encore.

Signe amoureux, duquel Amour s'honore,
Representant l'Androgyne lien,
Et le courroux du grand Saturnien,
Dont le nombril tousjours se rememore.

N'y ce beau chef, ny ces yeux, ny ce front,
Ny ce beau sein où les fleches se font,
Que les beautez diversement se forgent,

26

Pages 26–27 of *Florilège des Amours* by Pierre de Ronsard, published by Albert Skira, Paris, 1948. Lithograph, printed in color, page size 15 x 11½" (38.1 x 29.2 cm). Collection, The Museum of Modern Art, New York, Louis E. Stern Collection.

RIGHT:
Le Guignon, 1930–32, from *Poésies* by Stéphane Mallarmé, published by Albert Skira, Lausanne, 1932. Etching, printed in black, two pages, each 13 x 9¾" (33 x 24.8 cm). Collection, The Museum of Modern Art, New York; Louis E. Stern Collection.

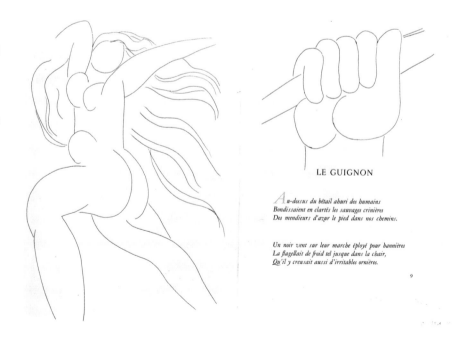

LE GUIGNON

aintenant, toi, approche, fraîchie sur
dès lits de violettes.

Moi, le roi aux cils épais, qui rêve dans le
désert ondulé.

moi, je vais rompre pour toi mon pacte fait
avec les bêtes,

et avec les génies noires qui dorment la nuque
dans la saignée

de mon bras, et qui dorment sans crainte que
je les dévore.

Des sources qui naissent dans tes paumes je
ne suis pas rassasié encore.

26

... fraîchie sur des lits de violettes...

"*...fraîchie sur des lits de violettes...*,"
pages 26–27 of *Pasiphaë/Chant de
Minos*, by Henri de Montherlant, pub-
lished by Martin Fabiani, Paris, 1944.
Linoleum cut, page size 12⅞ x 9⅞"
(32.7 x 25 cm). Collection, The
Museum of Modern Art, New York,
Louis E. Stern Collection.

The problem was exactly the opposite when he came to illustrate Henri de Montherlant's *Pasiphaë*. What to do so that the heavy black line of the linoleum cut would not pull down the rather empty page of text? Matisse's solution was to make one unit out of the double page and sur-round it with a margin of white. He said that when he first looked at the results he found the stark black and white a bit funereal. So after a good deal of thought—Matisse was anything but spontaneous—he decided to add "sparkle" by starting each page of text with a capital letter in red.

He spent years illustrating a great edition of the poetry of Ronsard, the French sixteenth-century poet who wrote so eloquently about love. Matisse worked on the *Florilège des Amours* with a care and precision that is hard to imagine. He chose the poems himself and was his own layout man. There is a series of albums in the Bibliothèque Nationale in Paris which shows all the different stages he went through. He tried and rejected many typefaces. He tried and rejected several kinds of paper. He modified and remodified his own designs. Finally, 126 lithographs were produced.

Florilège des Amours is an absolutely glorious book. Sometimes the ornamentation is just a grace note to the text. Sometimes Matisse threw an illustration over most of the page, leaving only a few lines of the poem.

I happened to be with him when he received his first copy of the book, and he was understandably delighted. He once said, "Can't one retain a young and ardent imagination? I feel better equipped to illustrate Ronsard's love poetry now than when I was twenty-five. Then, of course, I didn't need imagination."

One time, Matisse telephoned me in Paris and asked me to come to Vence; he had something to show me. I hurried down and found the old gentleman in bed, in the middle of his living room.

"I can't get up anymore," he said briskly, "so I had my bed moved to the largest room of the house, and I work here."

He was a benign figure of Edwardian elegance—there never was anything informal about Matisse—neatly dressed in a white shirt, turquoise sweater, and matching tie that brought out the blue of his eyes; he was carefully combed, his beard sculpted.

Matisse in bed with his first copy of *Florilège des Amours*, 1948. Photo: Clifford Coffin/Condé Nast.

Matisse in bed in his Vence living room, 1948. Photo: Clifford Coffin/Condé Nast.

There was a rose in a glass by his side, next to a characteristically rational piece of furniture he had designed himself: it consisted of a four-sided bed table with a number of shallow drawers, on a pivot. He could push it around to reach what he wanted, and outside each drawer was an offhand little drawing in white of what was inside. A brightly colored red and yellow blanket lay across his knees, and what with the arabesques of red iron scrolls at the foot of the bed, the whole scene was *très Matisse*.

The other end of the Vence living room, 1948. Photo: Clifford Coffin/Condé Nast.

Above his head was a frieze of brush-and-China-ink drawings of his granddaughter Jackie. At the opposite end of the living room, visible from his bed, were strips of brown paper pinned with colored shapes, climbing up the sides and covering the back wall, and charcoal sketches arranged with great precision. The red-and-white-striped armchair that can be seen in the small photograph on the left will be recognized by any Matisse admirer: it appears in a number of his paintings.

The master of the house was brandishing a large pair of scissors, and sheets of paper painted in solid bright colors were heaped in front of him. "I'm going to design a chapel," he said, and laughed at my outright astonishment. He was not known to be a practicing Catholic.

He told me how this had come about, and I believe I was the first person outside his immediate circle to hear his plans for what became the now famous Chapelle de Sainte-Marie-du-Rosaire at Vence.

When he had been so ill after his operation, Matisse had been nursed with exemplary devotion by a young woman who was planning to be a nun but had put off taking her vows until he was well on his way to recovery. She was, incidentally, a very pretty young woman, and had posed for Matisse several times. She then became a Dominican nun, taking the name Sœur Jacques. Matisse lost track of her. Much later he moved to Vence, and by an extraordinary coincidence, Sœur Jacques was sent there, to a rest home for Dominican nuns, not far from the Villa Le Rêve.

The nuns planned to build a small chapel to replace one that had burned down, and they needed a design for a stained-glass window. Sœur Jacques was considered to be "the artistic one," so she was asked to come up with a sketch. Matisse said his former nurse used to do watercolors, and sometimes he would show her his own work. She was frank. "The colors are very pretty . . . but it is not exactly the kind of thing I like." This delighted him. "You're the only one who tells me the truth!" he said. But Sœur Jacques had trouble with her stained-glass project, so she went to her former patient to get some advice. She had absolutely no idea of his worldwide reputation.

"What she had done was really very weak," Matisse told me, "but I didn't want to hurt her feelings." So he suggested that they send to Paris for some colored sheets of cellophane that could be cut and pasted into the model of the chapel she had made, to try out effects.

By the time the sheets arrived, Matisse's imagination had caught fire. The idea of the strong Midi sunlight pouring through stained-glass windows thrilled him. He could imagine the colored shadows they would throw—"a whole orchestra of colors," he said.

Soon he offered to do not one but all the windows, and then gradually he took over the design of the chapel itself, down to the smallest details—the altar, the crucifix, ceramic tile murals, even the vestments to be worn by the priests. The project captivated him.

It was an extraordinary example of a great artist becoming a painter, architect, designer, and sculptor all rolled into one. Here was the opportunity to fulfill an old ambition: to create a total environment. (He would have welcomed the opportunity to work on a large decorative project, for a public space, for instance, but no one—no governmental body, no private corporation—ever commissioned him.) He was to pour his entire time and enormous effort, not to mention some of his own money, into the chapel for four years. When we talked, it was just the beginning.

Since he wasn't able now to stand up to paint or draw, Matisse used his special *papier-découpé* [cut-paper] technique, one that he had used originally when he was working on his designs for the *Dance* mural for the Barnes Foundation in Merion, Pennsylvania, in 1931 (pages 90–91). He had Madame Lydia paint sheets of paper with brightly colored gouaches, all to his specifications. Then he would cut out shapes directly from the paper. There were no preparatory drawings. "I cut right into the chromatic mass," he said, "like a medieval sculptor carving into a block of stone." Next he would have Madame Lydia pin the shapes onto strips of brown paper, which represented the windows of the future chapel. From his bed Matisse could judge the effect and direct the modification of the arrangement.

Early maquettes show that he started out with the idea of geometric designs for the windows. But in the end he decided that leaf motifs would suit his purpose better. Of course, nothing was ever wasted with Matisse. His design of geometric shapes, called "The Bees," was given to a nursery school in his hometown in the north, and was made into a big wall of stained glass.

The chapel in Vence was to be white and black, with all the color concentrated in the windows. "You will see how the intensity of a single black line can balance the impact of the colored windows," he told me. (The principle of balancing one force against the other recurred constantly in Matisse's work.)

"On one wall I will place a ceramic mural of the Virgin and Child surrounded by flowers, very large" (ten by eighteen feet)—he showed me a drawing for this—"and on another, the Stations of the Cross. It will be most effective."

He went on to explain that he had to devise a special technique to

Matisse wielding his scissors, c. 1946.
Photo: Cameraphoto, Venice.

The Tree of Life, stained-glass windows in the Vence chapel, 202¾ x 99¼" (515 x 252 cm). Photo: Hélène Adant/Rapho.

make the huge-scale murals without getting out of bed. Once the preliminary drawings have led to the final designs, he said, "I will draw on squares of white tile that have been cooked once and coated with a special preparation. After my drawing, they will be cooked again, and the lines will be set permanently." (This was done the following year, 1949: working with a large brush, he painted heavy black lines on the tiles lined up on the floor.) "These squares will be small, easy to handle. Spread over the plaster walls, they will give a lively surface with a specific brilliance."

Matisse talked about his plans for the chapel with extraordinary enthusiasm. It was hard to realize that it was an old, bedridden man who was saying: "I'm going to make a church filled with gaiety, a place that will make people happy." I remember how young and fresh his voice sounded, and how animated.

The chapel was built several years later. Just as Matisse had planned it, when the sun pours through the chapel windows it throws pools of colored light onto the white marble floor and walls, light that is constantly in motion as the sun shifts. Matisse said he had considered the brilliant Midi sunlight as an element of building. For the windows he finally chose three colors: an intense blue, yellow, and green. He thought of them as the blue of the Mediterranean, the yellow of the sun, the green of the trees. And he restricted himself to leaf forms—philodendron and cactus. (Wherever Matisse lived and worked, he surrounded himself with a forest of plants.)

Fifteen windows, in tall, narrow panels, blaze in the south wall, facing the austere *Virgin and Child* ceramic mural. The *Stations of the Cross* are

Interior of the Vence chapel. Photo: Hélène Adant/Rapho.

White Chasuble, maquette, 1950–52. Collage: gouache on paper cutouts on canvas, 52⅜ x 78" (133 x 198 cm). Musée Matisse, Nice.

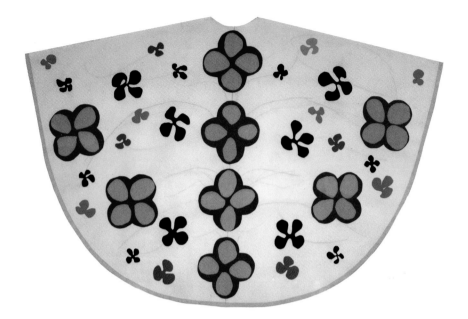

not placed around the chapel, as is customary, but grouped in a single panel on the back wall. The story of the Passion is told in a tense, abrupt shorthand that he achieved after many more literal preliminary drawings.

The altar designed by Matisse is placed at an unusual angle so that the officiating priest can be seen both by the congregation and by the Dominican nuns who sit tucked to one side in the choir stalls, also designed by Matisse. It's a very small chapel, with room for only about a hundred people.

To the right of the altar, Matisse placed another ceramic mural, more than fifteen feet high: the monumental, serene figure of St. Dominic, founder of the order. A well-known Dominican, Père Couturier, posed for this figure. He described to me how Matisse made drawing after drawing of him for more than an hour, chatting in a relaxed way. Suddenly the atmosphere changed. With great tension, in total silence, Matisse rapidly drew the definitive sketch—the accumulation of all that had gone before. Matisse so identified his model with this figure that he always referred to it as "Père Couturier" instead of St. Dominic.

Matisse told me that he considered the black-and-white habit worn by the Dominicans part of his decoration. But among the most beautiful designs he made for the chapel are the vestments to be worn for major religious feasts. The models were composed with cut-paper motifs, using simplified versions of Christian symbols. Picasso disapproved of the chapel on ideological grounds, but he so admired the vestments that he suggested Matisse design capes for bullfighters.

OPPOSITE:
Matisse and a Dominican priest in the Chapelle de Ste.-Marie-du-Rosaire, Vence. Photo: Hélène Adant/Rapho.

Rococo armchair in the collection of
the Musée Matisse, Nice.

Matisse was too unwell to go to the consecration of the chapel in June 1951, but he wrote to the bishop who officiated: "This work has taken me four years of exclusive and assiduous work and it represents the result of my entire active life. I consider it, in spite of its imperfections, to be my masterpiece."

There were efforts in certain circles to claim that Matisse's involvement with the chapel signified his return to the Church, but Matisse avoided any such commitment. He wrote that it was "an effort that stems from a life consecrated to the search for truth."

Fittingly, the road to the chapel was renamed avenue Henri Matisse.

Matisse stayed on for six years at the Villa Le Rêve, and then, in 1949, he moved back to his original apartment in Cimiez, which is where he died. After his death the family and the town of Nice wanted to make a little museum in his honor, to mark his presence in this part of the world that he had loved so much.

His own quarters weren't appropriate, so they took a late-seventeenth-century Italianate villa in Cimiez and made it over into a Matisse museum. It's very near an excavation of Roman thermal baths. The Romans were there in the third century, and I always thought Matisse would have liked the idea that beautiful Roman ladies had perhaps reclined in their baths right by his museum.

The Musée Matisse, with its enfilade of high-ceilinged rooms, red-tiled floors, white walls, and sparkling views over the treetops to the bay, is a thoroughly delightful place and a very touching one. A visit is like an invitation to see a family collection—most of what is on view was given by the artist's two sons and his daughter—and there are objects and pieces of furniture that meant a great deal to Matisse.

It has no pretension of being an ensemble of masterpieces, but the peaks are very high indeed. Matisse's son Jean left an important group of sculptures, and there are rich archives of graphic work and a very complete documentation of the Barnes *Dance* mural and the Vence chapel.

Certain of Matisse's possessions particularly stirred his imagination. He wrote of a rococo chair he acquired in 1941, "When I found it at an antique dealer's a few weeks ago, I was completely bowled over. It is splendid. I am obsessed by it." The chair was to appear in several paintings, and one of them—along with the chair itself—is in the museum.

Matisse, like Chardin, painted the same objects over and over—we find them in his still lifes—and even the same people, when possible. "I

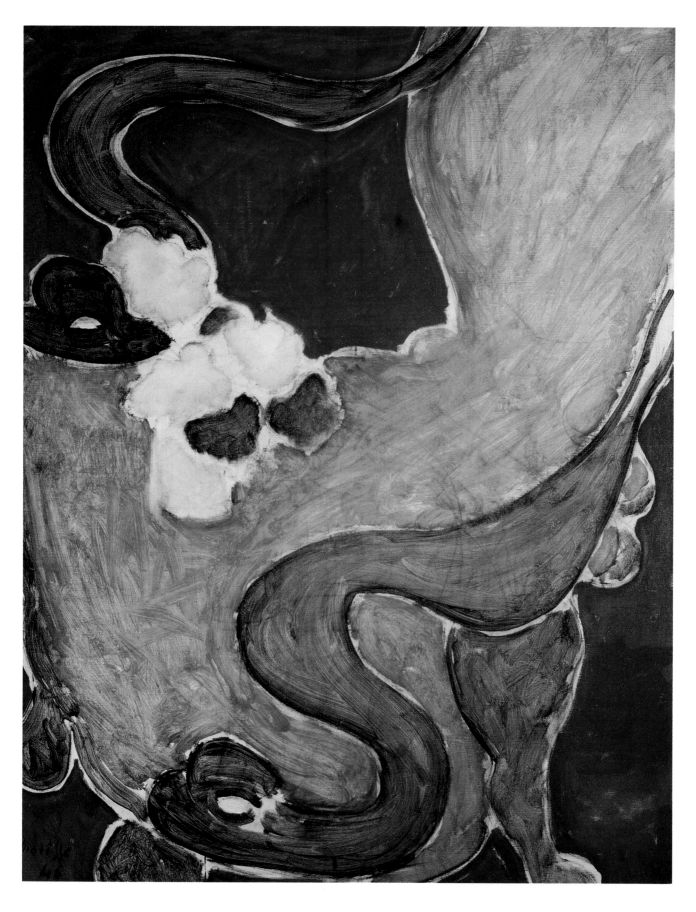

LEFT:

Pewter Jug, 1917. Oil on canvas, 36¼ x
25⅝" (92.1 x 56.1 cm). Baltimore
Museum of Art; Cone Collection,
formed by Dr. Claribel Cone and Miss
Etta Cone of Baltimore, Maryland.

RIGHT:

Pewter Jug, Lemons, and Chair, 1939.
Oil on canvas, 21⅝ x 18⅛" (55 x 46
cm). Private collection.

need," he said, "every day, to rediscover my idea of the day before." A
vitrine in the museum holds vases and jars that peopled his still lifes and
interiors for years. They are modest objects; he didn't look for the precious or the rare. There is a pewter jug, for instance, that appears in
paintings of 1917, 1939, and 1941.

Among the memorabilia are a stand Matisse used for his paintings and
palette, and a New Ireland figure that was part of his collection of prim-
itive objects. It once belonged to the French poet Paul Eluard, who was
a close friend of many of the best artists of the day. And besides several
violins, there are the Moroccan stove that appears often in his paintings
of odalisques, and the striped armchair that can be seen in the photograph of Matisse's Vence living room (page 42). There is also a luminous
blue ceramic fragment with a scrap of paper under it inscribed "From P
to M": it was a present from Picasso.

Matisse loved Cimiez. He found its light the most beautiful in the
world. He wrote a friend, "When I grasped I would be able to see
this light again and again every morning, I couldn't believe my good
fortune."

Except for the Vence years, from 1928 until he died Matisse lived and

Still Life with Magnolias, 1941. Oil on canvas. Musée National d'Art Moderne, Centre Georges Pompidou, Paris.

worked in a glass-and-stucco wedding-cake of an apartment building in Cimiez. (It was named La Régina, in honor of an earlier visitor, Queen Victoria, who used to spend winter holidays here; in those days no one thought of going to the south of France in summer.)

Here Matisse created surroundings that reflected his work in a series of mirror images: great plants in profusion, flowers everywhere, bowls of fruit, African masks, Polynesian necklaces . . . at one point there was a huge aviary filled with doves. And there were paintings by Courbet, Cézanne, Picasso.

By putting two of his ateliers together, Matisse had almost the exact dimensions of the little Vence chapel, so he could work here on his maquettes at almost full scale. When he was able to stand for short periods of time, he drew with charcoal attached to a long stick—as he had done for the Barnes mural. The photograph on page 52 shows him working on a half-scale model for the towering St. Dominic.

What started out as simply a convenient device—the use of *papiers découpés* for the Vence windows—led to a glorious new chapter of twentieth-century art: the enormous cut papers of Matisse's last years. They were a triumphant negation of pain and old age. When he could no longer stand up to work, he would sit in a wheelchair in the middle of a whirlpool of brilliant colors, planning his huge cut papers. When he had to take to his bed, he drew right on the wall and went on planning. He was stoic to the outer world about his physical disabilities, but as he wrote to a friend: "If only you knew the pent-up rages I sometimes get into when I feel this immobility forced upon me."

Sometimes he would sit in a chair, facing a *papier découpé* wall, to study it. The Cimiez studio-apartment was covered from floor to ceiling with cut papers; some were fixed to the walls, some trailed onto the floor. His bed was surrounded, too. "Now that I don't get up very often, I've made myself a little garden to go for walks in. Everything's there—fruit, flowers, leaves, a bird or two."

Above his head, he drew some larger-than-life heads of his grandchildren, in charcoal. "They keep me company, too. It was no trouble. I had

Matisse drawing with a stick in his Cimiez apartment, c. 1946. Photo: Robert Capa/Magnum.

Matisse in bed, drawing on the wall of
his Cimiez apartment, 1950. Photo:
Paris Match/Carone.

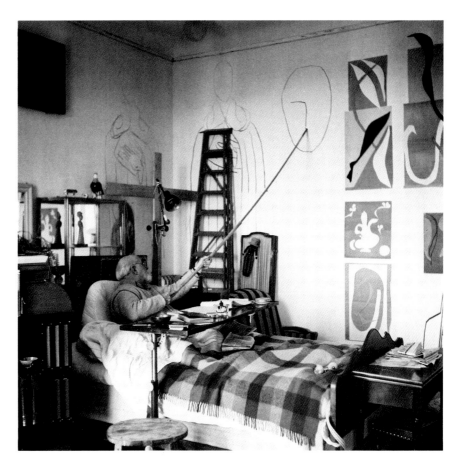

Large *papier découpé* on the wall of
Matisse's Cimiez apartment. Photographer unknown.

someone tie some charcoal to the end of that fishing rod there, and then I went to work." And sometimes his scissors conjured up a tall figure; but most often Matisse used the shapes of leaves and petals for his cut papers.

In 1952 he made a series of monochrome blue nudes, clearly related to his work in sculpture. "Instead of drawing a contour and filling it in with color, I draw directly into the color," Matisse said. He defined masses simply by leaving a narrow white space between them. *Blue Nude with Flowing Hair* sums up all that Matisse ever tried to say about the joy of the dance. With his scissors and paste, he could set a dancer free from the earth in a way that was not possible in oil paints on canvas. Here was levitation personified, a wingless creature that rivaled the birds in the sky.

Large Composition with Masks (page 56) is an immense composition,

Blue Nude II, 1952. Gouache on paper cutout, 45 ¾ x 35" (116.2 x 88.9 cm). Musée National d'Art Moderne, Centre Georges Pompidou, Paris.

H·MATISSE 52

more than thirty feet long. The repeated symmetric forms may look the same—leaves, petals, pistils—but they never are. In another, *The Parakeet and the Mermaid* (page 57), a sea siren is stranded in the topmost branches of a tropical forest. (The parakeet appears on the left.)

In his cut papers Matisse took the fat off art. The materials he used were weightless and incorporeal. They had extent, but not substance. There was nothing there until he put his shears to work. Yet drawing was never more drawing, and painting was never more painting, than in those late and last works. Their impact on younger painters was enormous.

Matisse would have liked some of his large *papiers découpés* such as these—environmental decorations, really—to be used in a public place. But, as we have seen, no one ever asked for them. John Russell wrote about the extraordinary experience it is to stand in front of these big cut-paper pictures, with the sheer size of their imagery, their physical scale: "These enormous pictures are like sighs of exhilaration as Matisse at last sighted the Promised Land: the complete simplification of painting."

In 1930 Matisse went to Tahiti, but contrary to what one might expect, he didn't paint there. "I'm no Gauguin," he said. The photographer Brassaï asked him why he didn't take more photographs of his trip. "Because I didn't want to freeze my impressions," Matisse answered. He spent much of his time swimming in the lagoon and noting the colors as sunlight, shining through the water, turned the bottom to absinthe.

He wrote that the light of the Pacific was intoxicating to the perception—it was like looking inside a golden cup. "The extraordinary day-

Large Composition with Masks, 1953. Collage: gouache on paper cutouts on canvas, 139¼ x 392½" (353.6 x 996.4 cm). National Gallery of Art, Washington, D.C.; Ailsa Mellon Bruce Fund.

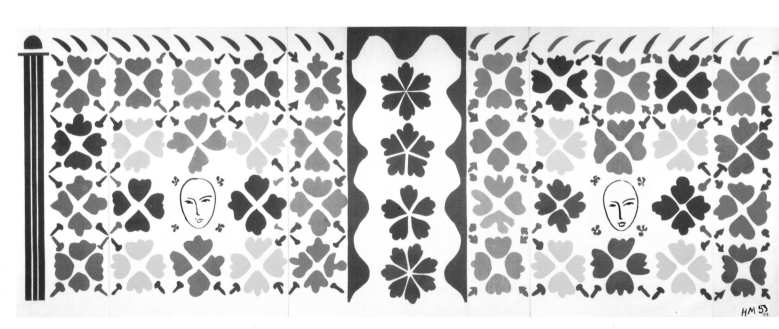

The Parakeet and the Mermaid, 1952. Collage: gouache on paper cutouts on canvas, 132 ¾ x 302½" (337 x 768.5 cm), six parts. Stedelijk Museum, Amsterdam.

light . . . the sky of an unknown substance, like precious stones. The water of an incredible richness around land that is orange, yellow, with some green."

More than twenty years later, Matisse distilled his memories and feelings in *Memory of Oceania* (page 58). He described *The Snail* (page 59), which he also called *Chromatic Composition*, as "an abstract panel taking its roots in reality." It is a chromatic display of uneven rectangles following a spiral movement—the nearest Matisse ever came to a non-objective art.

Here was pure color on its own, untrammeled, uncompromising, commanding attention to itself and for itself. Every painter today who uses color simply and directly is in some way indebted to Matisse.

Matisse used to go and see his old friend Tériade at Saint-Jean-Cap-Ferrat, not far from Cimiez. Tériade had a summer house there, the Villa Natasha. He was the publisher of the superb review called *Verve*, and he also published what is one of the most beautiful of all twentieth-century books, Matisse's *Jazz* (pages 103, 104).

At one time I used to spend part of every summer at Saint-Jean and I would visit Tériade. His terrace was the best place from which to watch the July 14 fireworks. Usually we dined in the garden—Tériade had what he described as the smallest dining room in the world. Matisse agreed. One day he said, "Really, Tériade, your dining room is too small. I'm going to open it up for you." So he followed the principles he had just

Memory of Oceania, 1952–53. Gouache
and crayon on paper cutouts over canvas, 112 x 112⅞" (284.4 x 286.4 cm).

Collection, The Museum of Modern
Art, New York; Mrs. Simon Guggenheim Fund.

The Snail, 1952. Gouache on paper
cutouts, 113 x 113⅜" (287 x 288 cm).
Tate Gallery, London.

tried out at the little Vence chapel, and designed a black-and- white ceramic mural and a strongly colored stained-glass window.

He made a cut-paper maquette for the window, called *Chinese Fish*. In his best professorial manner, Matisse pointed out that this was a real fish; he had found it in the Larousse dictionary.

The great French photographer Henri Cartier-Bresson took a picture of Matisse sitting in Tériade's garden. I always loved it, and was delighted when Cartier-Bresson gave me a print of it.

Matisse's son Pierre also had a house at Saint-Jean, and his father used to visit him there. When Pierre bought the house he liked everything about it except an ugly stained-glass window. "I'll fix that," his father said, and in 1953 he designed a window from a cut-paper maquette.

I often stayed with Pierre and his wife in Saint-Jean. As I watched the sun flooding the stairs with a pageant of color every afternoon, I often thought of the remarkable man who took a whole new lease on life through his late works. With his scissors and paste he painted big, he painted free, and he released an entirely new set of images.

He ought to have been dead, but he wasn't. He ought to have retired, but he hadn't. He looked all set to go on forever.

Yet when I asked him if he ever thought of going back to painting with oils and brushes, Matisse said: "Painting! I have plenty of time for that. After all, I'm only eighty-three!"

Matisse in the garden of Villa Natasha, 1951. Photo: Henri Cartier-Bresson/Magnum.

Conversation, 1909. Oil on canvas,
69 ⅝ x 85 ½" (177 x 217 cm). State
Hermitage Museum, Leningrad.

CHAPTER 2

Matisse the Inspired Conservative

Self-Portrait, 1937. Charcoal, 10 x 8″
(25.4 x 20.5 cm). Private collection.

Matisse was a revolutionary—a man who never stopped pushing out where no one had pushed out before. He was also an inspired conservative. The man who pushed is well known. Less so, the inspired conservative.

Matisse practiced a public art, and he never flunked a challenge on the grand scale. But he also practiced a private art. He made sculptures that he never thought of selling. He made prints by the score, and often nobody knew. He painted the same model over and over and over, obsessively.

Private himself, he had private people around him. His wife never talked about him. His children never talked about him. His models never talked about him. His true friend and closest assistant, Lydia Delektorskaya, never talked about him. I am going to try to break down a little of that privacy, although not—I hope—in ways that would make his eyes blaze and burn behind his thick glasses.

It was Matisse the inspired conservative who went in for sculpture. In sculpture, he was a plain man, a slow man, a man who modeled with clay in the traditional way. Not for him the constructions with which Picasso gave sculpture a whole new history. His themes were conservative, too: women standing up, women sitting down, women reclining.

Sculpture was his support and confidant at times when neither painting nor drawing nor printmaking could give him what he needed. Sculp-

Matisse with a piece of sculpture.
Photo: Robert Cohen/AGIP.

ture for him was a private activity, done for himself and with an explicit
purpose—to find a three-dimensional solution for problems that had
brought him to a standstill in painting. But again and again in his long life
he lived for sculpture, and it shows.

In his role as an inspired conservative, he knew from his many years
in the Louvre that more than one of the great French artists had used
sculpture as an intermediary in their paintings. Where the human figure
in painting is the three-dimensional thing that is arrested and made to
keep still, sculpture is the three-dimensional thing that is still by its very
nature. It is the standard of stillness, the paradigm of the third dimension.

Matisse lived with sculptures from the moment he first went to art
school. When he was in Gustave Moreau's class, and painted a view of it,

the plaster model kept the living model company. When he ran a school of his own in 1909, there was a plaster cast from the antique—the *Apollo Piombino*—to set off the living model. He drew from casts as a student and went on drawing from Greek sculpture in the Louvre when he was in his sixties.

His first sculptures were made in 1894. They were relief medallions, not only portable but pocketable, and for Matisse they had a secret meaning, in that the young woman portrayed was Caroline Joblaud, his mistress at the time.

Sculpture is slow work, but Matisse had a long patience, and sometimes he needed every bit of it. Two years of evening classes, with never a session missed, went into his variant of Antoine Barye's *Jaguar Devouring a Hare*. It was not simply that he looked and looked at the Barye. He also looked and looked at himself looking at the Barye. He wanted to get it right, in anatomical terms, but truth to his own feelings was every bit as important. (Matisse was a jaguar who kept his claws out of sight.)

The male human presence in general is rare in his paintings, and with one exception the broken-down male presence is unthinkable. In 1900, working from a model who had been a longtime favorite of Rodin's, he produced the *Male Model* (page 67), a painting that is Cézannesque in

Bronze relief medallion, 1894.

Matisse drawing from a Greek kouros in the Louvre, 1932. Photo: Pierre Matisse.

its idiom and Rodinesque in its overtones. Conceivably, he thought of it as a covert portrait of himself as a battered hero.

The sculptural version of the subject, known generally as *The Serf*, took him literally hundreds of sessions with the same model. Anatomical accuracy had to be combined with the surge and thunder of his own feelings. It was as if he had to dig into the mountain of manhood that stood before him, year after year.

To those who knew him late in his life as an Olympian figure, it is difficult to think of Matisse as an unfinished artist, let alone as an unfocused human being. But in 1903, when he was working on *The Serf*, he

RIGHT:
Matisse in his studio, with *The Serf*, c. 1908. Photographer unknown.

OPPOSITE:
Male Model, 1900. Oil on canvas, 39⅛ x 28⅝" (99.3 x 72.7 cm). Collection, The Museum of Modern Art, New York; Kay Sage Tanguy and Abby Aldrich Rockefeller Funds.

Henri Matisse Engraving, 1900–1903. Drypoint, printed in black, plate size 5 ⅜ x 7 ⅞ " (13.4 x 20 cm). Collection, The Museum of Modern Art, New York; Gift of Mrs. Bertram Smith.

made a self-portrait etching in which he looked like anxiety personified.

His plight was not imaginary, either. He had begun late. He was almost twenty-one before he held a brush in his hand, and he had shown no prior interest in art—or, for that matter, in anything else. He came from nowhere, and for quite some years he was nobody. His teachers discouraged him, almost without exception. Only Gustave Moreau, who had the touch of gold in such matters, said to him that he had been born to simplify painting.

In 1902, Matisse was in deep trouble financially, and he had to go back home to his family in a very grim part of northern France. Working in a long narrow room under the eaves, he nonetheless managed to suggest, perhaps unconsciously, that at the end of that long tunnel the Promised Land was waiting.

And he almost found it when he went to stay with his painter friend

Studio Under the Eaves, 1903. Oil on canvas, 21 ¾ x 18 1/8 " (55.2 x 46 cm). Fitzwilliam Museum, Cambridge, England.

Luxe, Calme, et Volupté, 1904. Oil on canvas, 38 3/4 x 46⅝" (98.3 x 118.5 cm). Musée National d'Art Moderne, Centre Georges Pompidou, Paris.

Paul Signac in Saint-Tropez in the summer of 1904. He loved the landscape, and the light, and Signac had persuaded him to work with quite another mode of painting. But somehow the picture that resulted, *Luxe, Calme, et Volupté*—the title taken from a poem by Baudelaire—doesn't come off, for all its historical importance. To me, it looks more as if sculpture were paying a call on painting and both sides were finding it rather sticky going.

The Serf is unique in Matisse's work in that it deals with the huge, grinding resentment, the physical and emotional deadlock, of aging manhood. Elsewhere, unblemished bodies were more his style. Privileged idleness and a certain vacancy of mind were more to his taste than the torment of a proletarian Atlas.

Still Life in Venetian Red, 1908. Oil on canvas, 35 x 41 ⅜" (89 x 105 cm). Pushkin State Museum of Fine Arts, Moscow.

Madeleine I, 1901. Bronze, cast # 3/10; 23 ¼ x 8 ¾ x 7 1/8" (59.1 x 18.1 cm). Baltimore Museum of Art; Cone Collection, formed by Dr. Claribel Cone and Miss Etta Cone of Baltimore, Maryland.

Even before *The Serf* was finished, Matisse began on female figures of that sort. As early as 1901 he made *Madeleine I*, which combined the serpentine or arabesque forms he always favored with the good big head of hair that particularly appealed to him. He kept these sculptures near him, as household pets that in due course would turn up in still-life paintings, just as sculptures turn up in masterpieces by Chardin and Cézanne. In 1908, Madeleine played her part against an Oriental carpet.

In March 1906, Matisse showed one of the most ambitious of all his paintings, his *Bonheur de Vivre*. Unless you go to the Barnes Foundation in Merion, Pennsylvania, near Philadelphia, you will never see it, as the Foundation does not allow its works to travel. Nor can you see it in color reproduction, because the Foundation doesn't allow them to be made. But Matisse's oil sketch for it, shown here, does suggest what this huge painting looks like.

There is a great deal to be said about the *Bonheur de Vivre*, not least regarding the use of figures taken directly from sculptures that Matisse had either made already or was about to make.

There is a group of dancing figures in the background. Matisse will reintroduce them later. They form the active, positive, Dionysiac element in the picture. The figures in the foreground look as if they have

Sketch for *Le Bonheur de Vivre*, 1905.
Oil on canvas, 18 x 23 ½" (45.7 x 59.7
cm). San Francisco Museum of Modern
Art, Elise S. Haas Collection.

TOP:
André Derain, *Portrait of Henri Matisse*,
1905. Oil on canvas, 18 1/8 x 13 ¾"
(46 x 34.9 cm). Tate Gallery, London.

BOTTOM:
Self-Portrait, 1906. Oil on canvas,
21 ⅝ x 18 1/8" (55 x 46 cm). Statens
Museum for Kunst, Copenhagen.

not quite made it from sculpture into painting. In fact, we could almost think that the picture represents a group of dancers whirling around and around in a sculpture garden. (In any case, we sense that Matisse wanted to put the potential of painting side by side with the potential of sculpture and see what came of it.)

What you cannot sense here is the intense emotional impact of the *Bonheur de Vivre*, which is roughly six feet high and eight feet wide and makes full use of the expressive force of Fauve painting. This is color of a power and eloquence that were new to painting at that time and have lost none of their strength and originality.

In Fauve painting, color was freed from the drudgery of description and allowed to go its own way. It was about feeling, as much as—or more than—it was about fact. In Matisse's 1905 landscapes, tree trunks are red at the bottom and turn blue higher up. Orange, purple, and violet turn up where we never expect them in nature, and yet we believe in them. In the same way, we believe that the famous *Woman with a Hat* had to be a disciplined riot of color, even if we know that when Madame Matisse posed for it she wore a black hat, a black dress, and black gloves. We accept it as the only way in which Matisse could have released his feelings about his wife, about the present state of painting, and about himself.

André Derain was one of the Fauve pioneers. When he first got to know Matisse he tried to infect him with something of his own boisterous physicality. "He looked ten years younger when I'd finished with him," Derain said afterwards. His 1905 portrait of Matisse has a distinctly wistful look, but by the summer of 1906, when Matisse painted another self-portrait, there did seem to be a radical change. The tall pointed profile of the eyelids and the huge, all-seeing eyes were studied almost as searchingly as Cézanne studied himself. We recognize Matisse as a man who would dare anything in his art.

Matisse had a dialogue going on between his painting and his sculpture, and in 1906 he more than once took figures from his *Bonheur de Vivre* and turned them into small sculptures. In dealing with the human figure he was a close-up man, rather than a middle-distance man. He liked healthy young bodies that stuck out here and there, and he didn't mind if awkwardness resulted. As he pushed and pinched and squeezed the clay, he never thought to smooth out the impact of his fingers and thumbs. These were his marks, and he stood by them.

In some of his big subject paintings of 1907, Matisse gave the figures an urbane smoothness and roundness of silhouette. But where the input of sculpture was decisive, as it was in the big *Blue Nude* of that year (page 12), the image took on a pitiless quality that was to outrage the American public in 1913. He himself said that the dialogue between painting and sculpture was particularly intense in the case of the *Blue Nude* and the bronze *Reclining Nude I.*

When Matisse was really possessed by one of his sculptures, he didn't like to let it go. Doubtless the charm was all the more potent when the pose had erotic connotations that went back to Roman times. Be that as it may, he gave the *Reclining Nude* of 1906–07 a second life in 1908, in a painting where it looked almost, but not quite, like flesh and blood.

By 1908, Matisse knew that it was time for him to come forward with a major statement in painting. He had to do it. There was a general sense that the future of progressive art lay with Cubism, and in particular with Picasso. Picasso's *Woman with a Fan* (page 74) had a direct, frontal, unhesitating

ABOVE:
Reclining Nude I, 1906–07. Bronze, 13½ x 19¾ x 11¼" (34.3 x 50.2 x 28.6 cm). Collection, The Museum of Modern Art, New York; Acquired through the Lillie P. Bliss Bequest.

RIGHT:
Sculpture and a Persian Vase, 1908. Oil on canvas, 23¾ x 29" (60.5 x 73.5 cm). Nasjonalgalleriet, Oslo.

OPPOSITE:
Pablo Picasso, *Woman with a Fan*,
1908. Oil on canvas, 59⅞ x 39¾"
(152 x 101 cm). State Hermitage
Museum, Leningrad.

ABOVE:
Bathers with a Turtle, 1908. Oil on
canvas, 70½ x 86¾" (179.1 x 220.3
cm). St. Louis Art Museum; Gift of Mr.
and Mrs. Joseph Pulitzer, Jr.

Sergei Shchukin, 1912. Charcoal, 19½ x
12" (49.5 x 30.5 cm). Private collection.

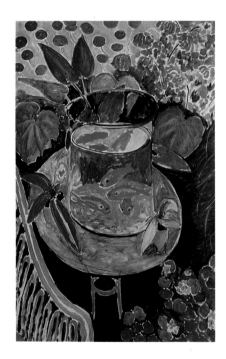

Goldfish, 1911. Oil on canvas, 57⅞ x
38⅝" (147 x 98 cm). Pushkin State
Museum of Fine Arts, Moscow.

attack. It drew on primeval sources of feeling. It was about power,
authority, and an unrelenting fate.

Matisse's *Bathers with a Turtle* (page 75) was also an extraordinary
picture, played out on a perfectly flat ground that consisted simply of
three horizontal bands of close-hued color. But there was something
curiously awkward, hesitant, and uneven about it. More than forty years
later, Matisse admitted to a friend: "When Cubism was at the forefront
of the art stage, that was a difficult time for me."

Picasso's *Woman with a Fan* was bought by a man from Moscow who
for ten years had been building up a collection of French avant-garde
paintings far superior to any other. His name was Sergei Shchukin. His
town house in Moscow had better recent paintings, and more of them,
than any European museum. People went from Paris to Moscow
expressly to see his Monets. He also had major works by Cézanne,
Degas, Renoir, Gauguin, van Gogh, and others. By 1914 he owned fifty
paintings by Picasso and thirty-eight by Matisse.

On his scouting trips in Paris, Shchukin got to know about Matisse.
Matisse, for his part, knew that anyone who could buy Cézanne's
Woman in Blue and Monet's *Woman in a Garden* was no ordinary collector. Besides, Shchukin was an immensely wealthy merchant. When he
began to buy Matisse's paintings, the artist must have taken it as a sign
from heaven.

In spite of his timid manner, Shchukin had an intrepid instinct that led
him to buy startling and innovative works like the *Harmony in Red,*
which Matisse produced in 1908. Shchukin was all the braver in that
when he chose the painting in Paris it was a harmony in blue-green.
After the sale was made, Matisse decided that a crimson-cinnabar would
give the painting the unity he wanted, and he went ahead and changed
it completely. Shchukin took it in his stride. It now has a huge, all-
enveloping authority that is masked by what looks at first like conventional subject matter.

Matisse was still reluctant to abandon the bourgeois interior, and he
was also reluctant to abandon the figure of Caroline Joblaud, who reap-
pears after a ten-year absence as the submissive angel of the house.

By the way, Matisse really did have a heavy, figured piece of material
like that in *Harmony in Red.* But it wasn't red; it was blue. It serves as a
background in more than one still life between 1909 and 1919.

Shchukin also latched onto the *Goldfish* of 1911. In North Africa,
Matisse had been both fascinated and puzzled by the way Moroccans
would gaze at goldfish in their bowls, hour after hour. Something of

their hypnotized interest must have rubbed off on him; he was to paint a number of pictures in which goldfish were major players. Matisse identified with them in a way peculiar to himself. Goldfish looked out on the world through glass. They were in it, and yet not of it. A painter friend once said of Matisse: "Of course, he's quite inhuman, like a goldfish looking out on the world." He was very conscious of his feelings, and when toward the end of his life a visitor admired a green stem that was standing in water he said: "Yes. It makes me want to be a vermilion goldfish."

Perhaps the greatest service Shchukin rendered to Matisse was the invitation to paint mural decorations for his house in Moscow. Early in 1909, Matisse showed Shchukin the big painting called *Dance* (page 78), now in the Museum of Modern Art in New York. Matisse loved the dance, though I doubt that he himself would have made the chorus line. The dance was not, as he saw it, something you bought tickets to see in

Harmony in Red, 1908. Oil on canvas, 70⅞ x 78¾" (180 x 200 cm). State Hermitage Museum, Leningrad.

Dance (first version), 1909. Oil on
canvas, 102½ x 153½" (260.4 x 389.9
cm). Collection, The Museum of
Modern Art, New York; Gift of
Nelson A. Rockefeller in honor of
Alfred H. Barr, Jr.

Dance (second version), 1909–10. Oil
on canvas, 102 ⅜ x 154" (260 x 391
cm). State Hermitage Museum,
Leningrad.

Foot, 1909. Bronze, height 11 ¾" (30 cm).

a theater. It was the embodiment of the Dionysiac element in life that he liked to watch on Sunday afternoons at the Moulin de la Galette in Paris, where young people would join hands and fling themselves around to the music of the farandole.

Nearly nine feet high and thirteen feet wide, *Dance* was one of Matisse's great undertakings. And of course the flatness, the minimal modeling, and the expressive distortions made an unprecedented effect. At first sight, it looks like a picture in which neither time nor place plays any part. Who are these pale-skinned people, and why are they dancing forever on top of a green hill with a huge blue sky behind them? The distant ring of dancers in his 1906 *Bonheur de Vivre* had been plucked out of the background and blown up to heroic proportions.

Shchukin was game for anything, especially after a very good lunch at Larue—one of the best restaurants in Paris—and he agreed to commission both an identical-size version of *Dance* and a companion piece, *Music*.

It was typical of Matisse that even when he was given the go-ahead for what might have been an exact replica of *Dance*, he made a new *Dance* (page 79) that was really not at all like the first version. It was the same size, but the pale skins were lobstered. The cheerful round dance had turned into a test of endurance. Bodies were convulsed and frantic, with every twist and turn spelled out. It was almost a foretaste of Stravinsky's *Rite of Spring*, where the dance ends in death. The use of strong red against green and blue over a huge area redoubled the intensity of the basic image.

And it was also typical of Matisse that he turned to his old confidant, sculpture, to help him amend and improve the new painting. The dancing figures might look as if they were going to lift off at any moment, but Matisse the inspired conservative was going to see to it that their ringleader, the dancer on the extreme left, had his foot firmly planted on the ground in correct anatomical style. Matisse went about it as carefully as if he were in medical school; hence the study of the foot.

Matisse rarely threw anything away, and when he came to paint *Music*, as the pendant to Shchukin's *Dance*, he looked back to a painting done in 1907. It shows a dancing couple, a figure rapt in daydream, and a standing violinist. The dancing couple have the timeless abandon that we also find in Edvard Munch's paintings of young people dancing by the sea. The seated figure, stilled and quiet, is lost in music. As for the violinist, he is the prime mover in a scene that, without him, would not exist. Yet he takes no part in it.

ABOVE:
Music, 1910. Oil on canvas, 102 ⅜ x
153 1/8" (260 x 389 cm). State Hermitage Museum, Leningrad.

RIGHT:
Sketch for *Music*, 1907. Oil on canvas,
29 x 24" (73.4 x 60.8 cm). Collection,
The Museum of Modern Art, New
York; Gift of A. Conger Goodyear in
honor of Alfred H. Barr, Jr.

Violinist at the Window, 1917. Oil on canvas, 58⅝ x 38⅜" (149 x 97.5 cm). Musée National d'Art Moderne, Centre Georges Pompidou, Paris.

It may well be relevant that Shchukin would have seen this painting at Gertrude and Leo Stein's when he was in Paris. In any case, Matisse, with true French thrift, was able to distill both *Music* and *Dance* from it.

Matisse himself played the violin. (His violin and/or its case appear in a number of his canvases.) Although he started relatively late in life, he saw no reason why—if he applied himself to music as he had to art—he would not really get somewhere.

Pierre Matisse described to me how his father's relentless practicing drove the family crazy. Matisse would take refuge in the bathroom for these sessions, hoping no one would hear him there. When young Pierre made the mistake of expressing interest in the violin, it unleashed a torrent. Papa Matisse took him out of school, had him tutored in violin, piano, and solfège. "It never occurred to him that if I had not already mastered these disciplines at sixteen, it was hopeless. Besides, I had no talent. Finally," Pierre added, "I was saved by World War I. I got conscripted."

Music was quite a new challenge for Matisse. It had to be a companion for the second *Dance*—same size, same number of people, same generalized location, same generalized tonalities. But it also had to be the absolute antithesis of *Dance*—a scene in which nobody moves and everyone has his two feet on the ground.

Matisse had trouble with *Music*, and we know from a photograph of the work in progress that at one time he wanted to furnish it not only with indications of spring but, in one version, with a large dog. (He also planned to have the musicians take their cue from the violinist, who would turn toward them as if giving the downbeat.)

Perhaps he thought that was too fussy. In the final version, nobody looks at anybody else. All face us, rapt, unstirring, and largely sexless. As has often been said, the five figures look like a metaphor for the rise and fall of notes on a page of music. Matisse here says everything, and says it with almost nothing.

When *Dance* and *Music* were shown in Paris before going to Moscow, they caused a terrible outcry. Shchukin began to get cold feet. The cartoonists got busy, too, and *La Vie Parisienne* published parody drawings called "Before" and "After," in which the five woebegone figures on a bare mountain were turned into bacchantes by a magnum of the right stuff. Shchukin wasn't easily panicked, but this time he nearly ran for cover.

To his credit, Shchukin held firm and braved Moscow bourgeois public opinion by installing the controversial panels. And he went on buying

HENRI MATISSE : *Avant.*

HENRI MATISSE : *Après.*

"Before" and "After" from *La Vie Parisienne*, October 8, 1910. (Reproduced in Jack Flam, *Matisse: The Man and His Art 1869–1918*, Cornell University Press, 1986).

the largest and grandest of Matisse's paintings as they came along. Naturally enough, he was delighted with the 1912 *Nasturtiums with "Dance,"* which included a version of *Dance* as a glamorous background.

Occasionally Shchukin took his time. In 1909 Matisse painted the monumental *Conversation* (page 62), which is now generally regarded not only as a portrait of himself and his wife, but as a landmark in the portrayal of matrimonial crisis. But it was not until 1912 that Shchukin wrote to Matisse that he couldn't get the painting out of his mind. Such were the richness and the profundity of its color, he said, that it reminded him of a Byzantine enamel. Finally, he couldn't resist it.

From one stupendous year, 1911, Shchukin bought two very large

The Pink Studio, 1911. Oil on canvas, 70⅝ x 87" (179.5 x 221 cm). Pushkin State Museum of Fine Arts, Moscow.

The Painter's Family, 1911. Oil on canvas, 56⅜ x 76⅜" (143 x 194 cm). State Hermitage Museum, Leningrad.

paintings that complemented one another both in their extreme complication and in their presentation of Matisse's life in Issy-les-Moulineaux, near Paris.

Throughout his life, the studio was not only the most important place in his life but, in a true sense, the only place that he took seriously. In *The Pink Studio* (page 83)—the studio was in reality a prefabricated hut, of a kind recommended to him by the American photographer Edward Steichen, and not pink at all, by the way—Matisse gave a concise runthrough of what he had been doing in painting and sculpture in the previous few years, together with a hint of what he was going to do. We feel that his real family, the one that he thought about in his every waking moment, was his art.

Glorious as *The Painter's Family* is, we wonder if the virtuoso patterning and texture is not the real subject of the picture. And, as Jack Flam has pointed out, we cannot help noticing how a cast of his sculpture *The Serf* glares down on the room from the chimneypiece. The implication may be that while the rest of the family were doing nothing much, Matisse was serving a life sentence of continual hard labor.

If he did think that, it was with some reason. Year after year he was breaking the mold of painting, feeling his way into a severity of statement that was entirely his own. In 1914, he painted one of his plainest and yet most audacious pictures, *The Open Window*. The theme of the open window was a lifelong favorite with Matisse, but in this case he took out all the things that normally he most loved to put in. All we see is a tall black rectangle in the middle, a beat-up green shutter on the left, and a beat-up blue wall on the right. It is for us to figure out where we are. Matisse isn't telling.

In *Artist and Goldfish*, also of 1914, we have no trouble seeing the goldfish, but Matisse has reduced himself to a palette, a thumb, and a schema of straight lines, filled in with areas of black, white, blue, and pink that are as near to abstraction as he ever got. It is as if he emptied himself out of the picture. (Vanished likewise is the companionable jumble of seductive objects in which he usually set his goldfish bowl.) Everything is stark, grim, linear.

Shchukin didn't buy paintings only by Matisse. But by his consistent

LEFT:

The Open Window, 1914. Oil on canvas, 45⅞ x 34⅝" (116.5 x 88 cm). Musée National d'Art Moderne, Centre Georges Pompidou, Paris.

RIGHT:

Artist and Goldfish, 1914. Oil on canvas, 57¾ x 44¼" (146.5 x 112.4 cm). Collection, The Museum of Modern Art, New York; Gift of Florene M. Schoenborn and Samuel A. Marx (the former retaining a life interest).

Bathers by a River, 1916. Oil on canvas, 102¼ x 153½" (259.7 x 389.9 cm). Art Institute of Chicago; Charles H. and Mary F. S. Worcester Collection.

support and encouragement he enabled Matisse to make other great paintings on the grand scale. Sometimes, as with the 1916 *Bathers by a River*, they took him years to complete. Sometimes, as with *The Moroccans* (page 13), also of 1916, they were worked up from memory with an exceptional freedom and complexity of reference. In both paintings there is a total aloofness from what anyone else was doing. There is also a sense of majesty, as if Matisse at last felt free to reorder the world as he wished.

It was until lately the received wisdom that when Matisse went to live mainly in Nice, from 1916 on, he took things easy and in general opted out of the struggle. That was never quite true of the paintings in question, and it was certainly not true of the sculptures that he made in the 1920s. The truth is that he worked as hard as ever, but that not all of it showed.

Michelangelo is somewhere behind the large seated nude sculpture that Matisse produced in 1925. Matisse the inspired conservative had

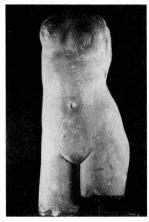

been drawing as assiduously from a cast after Michelangelo in Nice as if he had been a beginner, instead of a great artist in his fifties.

But this is a sculpture that is very much of its own time. Whereas in painting his Nice odalisques Matisse often worked with models that were yielding, pulpy, and full of spread, the *Large Seated Nude* was squared off with the knife until the figure was full of straight, flat forms and a silhouette that was all muscle. She is a young sportswoman of the mid-twenties.

Matisse could work on a very large scale, but he was every bit as inventive when the end result was exactly three inches high. He owned a Roman copy of a Greek marble fragment of the fourth century B.C., which he distilled down, in his thoughts, to one-eighth of its actual size. Then he went to work on a sculpture of his own.

The year after he made that tiny torso, 1930, Matisse came to the United States—on his way to Tahiti—as a member of the Carnegie International Prize jury. He himself had won the first prize in 1927 with a sumptuous still life. This time he saw to it that the prize went to Picasso, for his classic portrait of his wife. Matisse was taken on a tour of American collections, and the legendary and irascible Dr. Albert C. Barnes invited him to come and see his pictures in Merion.

After the tour was over—and Matisse was duly impressed, perhaps not

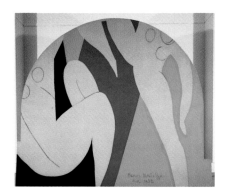

TOP:
Dance I, right section, 1931–32. Oil on canvas, 139 ¾ x 196" (355 x 498 cm). Musée d'Art Moderne de la Ville de Paris.

BOTTOM:
Dance II, right section, 1931–32. Oil on canvas, 147 ⅝ x 185" (375 x 470 cm). Barnes Foundation, Merion, Pennsylvania. Photo © Barnes Foundation.

least by his own *Bonheur de Vivre*—Dr. Barnes asked him abruptly if he would paint a mural for the main gallery, up in the space filled by three lunettes above a bank of windows.

This was a daunting proposition. The space in question was eighteen feet above the gallery floor, and would have to be seen from below. The lunette arches would interrupt the mural. Light coming through the windows would distract. And below were some of the greatest paintings of the previous fifty years—among them Cézanne's big *Cardplayers*, Seurat's *Poseuses*, Matisse's own *Riffian*, and a big Picasso. Who would want to mess with all that?

Matisse didn't say yes, but he didn't say no, either. He went back to Nice to think it over. After a second visit to Merion, he accepted the challenge. In Nice, in 1931, he rented an industrial space that was big enough for him to work on the decoration at full monumental scale. And twenty years after his panel for Shchukin he decided to go back to the theme of the dance.

As can be seen in the photograph on page 89, he drew with a piece of charcoal attached to a long stick. To avoid the fatigue of climbing up and down a ladder all the time to judge the effect of colors, he had assistants take pieces of paper that he had already painted and pin them onto places he indicated on the canvas. This device was to grow from a working practice to a glorious end in itself: the exhilarating cut-paper compositions of his last years.

Later Matisse described his method: "For years I worked like this, constantly rearranging eleven flat, colored shapes, rather like moving counters in a game of checkers . . . until I found an arrangement that satisfied me completely." Then he carried out the results in oil on canvas.

For the Moscow panels of *Dance* and *Music*, he had simplified composition and colors. Now, with a mural in mind, he pushed his ideas even further. On such a scale—the final panel was about forty feet long—information must be reduced to a minimum and details eliminated. "A hand indicates the way less effectively than an arrow," he said.

From the start, Matisse thought of his decoration as a fragment of architecture. "Architectural painting," he said, "must give to the space enclosed by the architecture a total atmosphere comparable to a vast, beautiful, sunny glade that surrounds the spectator with refreshment."

Colors must be kept down, to associate tactfully with the severity of stone and concrete. He saw that with color relationships it is quantity that makes quality. By understanding that the size of a work is a determining factor he showed how ahead of his time he was.

RIGHT:
Sketch of *Dance*, inscribed to Lydia
Delektorskaya, 1934.

BELOW:
Matisse drawing the *Dance* panel, photographed by Lydia Delektorskaya.

Dance II, 1931–32. Oil on canvas, 151⅝ x 187", 157½ x 196⅞", 147⅝ x 185" (385 x 475 cm, 400 x 500 cm, 375 x 470 cm). Barnes Foundation, Merion, Pennsylvania. Photo © Barnes Foundation.

Lydia Delektorskaya at work, photographed by Matisse.

In fact, Matisse foresaw that "one day easel painting will no longer exist, because of changing ways. There will be mural painting." And this was more than half a century ago.

After laboring for an entire year on the Barnes commission, he completed it only to find out that he had been working to the wrong measurements. Probably any other artist would have simply modified his first composition, but not Matisse. Working through a second year, he altered his scheme to include eight figures instead of the original six. They seem to have expanded in size and energy, and they practically leap and tumble out of their allotted space. No reproduction can convey the exuberance of Matisse's dancers. They must be seen *in situ* at the Barnes Foundation.

The effort of the Barnes decoration was so exhausting that after overseeing its installation, Matisse had to go off to Abano Terme, an Italian spa, for a cure, and he did not paint for nearly a year. But then he resumed work on the first version, which is now in the Petit Palais in Paris.

One of the best things that ever happened to Henri Matisse was that in 1932 a young White Russian woman named Lydia Delektorskaya came to help him, in Nice, with his Barnes mural.

Born in Siberia, the daughter of a doctor, she had lost her parents in

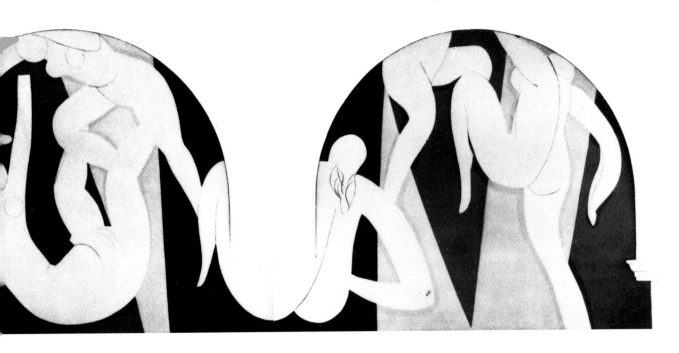

the typhoid and cholera epidemics of the early twenties. She arrived in France as a refugee, alone, penniless, not knowing a word of French.

After six months, when Matisse had finished the mural, there was no need for her to stay, and she left. Before very long Madame Matisse, a semi-invalid, needed someone as nurse and paid companion. They thought of Lydia and asked her to come. She said yes, and in October 1933 she came to the house; until the day of Matisse's death in 1954 she never left his side. (Eventually her presence and the predominant role she played in Matisse's life caused Madame Matisse to leave the house. The break was irreparable.)

It never entered Lydia's head that Matisse might want to hire her as a model. She was very much not Matisse's type. He had always worked with dark, southern models, and she was the very apotheosis of the unforgettable blonde. But after about a year, she sensed that Matisse was beginning to look at her with more and more interest. She thought nothing of it. And then one day, when she had unconsciously taken up a rather lazy, nonchalant pose, he said, "Don't move!" and began to draw her.

From that day on, she was indispensable to him—first as model, and eventually as studio assistant and archivist. He loved to photograph her, too. She knew nothing about art. She had no idea what artists were like, and she was surprised and rather shocked to find that when Matisse was working hard he used the most appalling language. "What a goddamn

way to earn a living!," he would say over and over, and you can believe
me that that was the least of it.

When he saw that she didn't like it, he tried to stop. But the next
morning he would go ahead just the same, and after the twenty-first bad
word she realized that she would just have to live with it. In fact, she
came to recognize it as a mark of the extreme nervous tension that over-
came Matisse when he got down to work. When he had taken a clean
new canvas and decided on his subject he would often sit for ten minutes
or more, speechless and motionless, looking closely at the white surface
in front of him. Then he would get up and say, "I just have to smoke a
cigarette." More than once, he would scrutinize the subject, raise his
hand, point his index finger at the canvas, and trace in the air the outline
of what he wanted to do. Then he would let his arm drop and say, "Damn
it! If only I'd had a brush in my hand, the thing would be done by now!"

Lydia reported that when his Dominican friend Père Couturier came
to have his portrait drawn for the ceramic mural in the Vence chapel,
Matisse got into such a terrible state that Père Couturier said, "You
really shouldn't get so exasperated, you know." And Matisse said, "I'm
not exasperated! I've got stage fright." On that same day he said that
when he made portraits he identified so strongly with the sitter that he
no longer knew what he was doing. "It's as if I was emptied out," he said,

"and was just watching myself at work." Did he feel the same way about drawing a leaf or a flower? "Exactly the same," he said.

Lydia also noticed that Matisse liked to get as close as possible to the model. Hissing and cursing, a mere six feet away, he must have been an intimidating sight. But he defended his position.

"It's like when you pass a cake shop," he said. "If you see the cakes through the window, they may look very nice. But if you go inside the shop and get them right under your nose, one by one, *then* you're in business!"

In Lydia's photograph albums, which have been published in Paris, we have an exact record of the paintings Matisse made between 1934 and September 1939. Quite often he made notes on the back of the photographs about the colors he had used.

Lydia also took photographs, almost hour by hour when the occasion called for it, that now have a great fascination for us as proofs of exactly how Matisse went to work. Her series documenting the large *Pink Nude*

Reclining Nude, 1936. Charcoal. 13 x 19⅝" (33 x 50 cm). Private Collection.

TOP:
Matisse with the model for *The Reader at the Table*, Henriette Darricarrère, 1921. Photo: Man Ray.

BOTTOM:
Matisse with an unidentified model, 1939. Photo: Brassaï.

of 1935 (which is now in the Baltimore Museum of Art) shows how often Matisse shifted the position of the model until he was completely satisfied.

But of course (and although she would dismiss the idea out of hand) we are immensely interested and moved to see what he made of her dur-

Lydia, photographed by Matisse,
c. 1935.

ing the years when she was his first inspiration and he clearly couldn't get enough of her as a model (pages 92–94).

He began quite decorously, and when he gave her a drawing it was inscribed very formally to "Madame Lydia Delektorskaya" (page 89). But as time went on she became the subject of some of the most voluptuous of all his drawings. He always liked to say that a naked model meant no more to him than a spoon or a fork, but in this case I don't believe it. Even his photographs of Lydia have a charge of feeling that is unmistakable.

I should say here that Lydia is one of the most undemanding and self-sufficient people who ever lived. She lived on nothing then, and she lives on nothing now, and anyone who thinks that she will accept as much as a cup of coffee from people who come to ask her about Matisse is greatly mistaken. After he died, she gave what she owned of his work to the great Russian museums where he is so richly represented.

Lydia was essential to Matisse throughout the long and glorious final phase of his career. When he was progressively more immobilized after his operation in March 1941, it was she who placed the pieces of cut and painted paper under his direction. Every day, all day, she was with him when he was at work, and for many years after his death it was she who was asked to restore the works whose development she had witnessed in their every detail.

On the way to Tahiti in 1930, Matisse stopped in New York and visited his son Pierre, who had just established himself there as an art dealer. Matisse *père* was crazy about New York: "Since arriving here I feel twenty years younger." He couldn't get over what he spoke of as the intensity of the very pure, crystalline light, the sense of space in the city, its architecture—he even liked the traffic lights. He spent three hours at the Met, he sketched at the zoo.

Matisse spoke in wonder of the "sheer immense size of America" and added: "If I were thirty, this is where I would come to work. There's so much energy in everything." Half seriously, he spoke of just staying there and not going any farther.

He did, of course, go on with his journey.

When Matisse arrived in the United States, a reporter asked him why he was going to Tahiti. "To see its light," he answered. So the reporter wrote: "Famous artist leaves wife and family to follow in Gauguin's footsteps," and more of the same. When Matisse came back to America he

Matisse on a New York City rooftop, 1930. Photo: Pierre Matisse.

Tahitian coconut palms, photographed by Matisse, 1930.

OPPOSITE, TOP:
Trees in Tahiti, 1930. Pen and ink.
Musée Matisse, Nice.

OPPOSITE, BOTTOM:
Trees in Tahiti, 1930. Pen and ink.
Musée Matisse, Nice.

ran into the same reporter. "You're the wretch who wrote such lies about me," he fumed.

The reporter answered, "But Mr. Matisse, put yourself in my place. If I had written that you just went to look at the light, there would have been no story, and I would have been fired!"

As you will have realized by now, Matisse was a careful man. There were subjects about which he wouldn't say a word, even if you prized open his mouth with a spoon. One of them was his visit to Tahiti. When pressed to say something about it, he went along with the tourist brochures and said that it was an island where indolence and pleasure reigned, thought was banished, and the future was forgotten.

When he drew in Tahiti, which was not often, he drew as a traveling botanist might have done it, to set down the look of trees that he might never see again. "When you draw a tree you must feel yourself growing with it," he used to say.

(As for the frangipani and pandanus, their perfume reminded him of good bread fresh from the oven. He never forgot them.)

Beyond that—well, no, he said, he hadn't taken photographs, because he had not wanted to fix his impressions. As a matter of fact he did take some photographs, which have surfaced only recently. They are not masterpieces, but they catch the thrust of the coconut palms. "Those palms go up so fast," Matisse said, "that you can't believe they'll ever stop." And he wrote to Pierre Bonnard: "A good stay, a good rest. Have seen all kinds of things. Will tell you all about them. Spent twenty days on a coral island: pure light, pure air, pure color—diamond, sapphire, emerald, turquoise. Extravagant fish. Have done absolutely nothing but take bad photos."

He swam a lot, and looked at the seabed through the glass bottom of a boat, and drew a bit from his hotel balcony. He didn't mind looking at sailboats at anchor, the trees that framed the view, and the island of Moorea in the background. But when he saw Tahitians standing around in Gauguinesque costumes and attitudes, he couldn't get away fast enough. "Pictorially speaking," he said, "Tahiti means nothing to me."

The truth is that Tahiti was a gigantic experience, and just too big to talk about as yet. But when he was asked in 1935 to design a tapestry, he chose a plain, careful account of the view from his Tahitian hotel window. He played with it a bit and finally sent in a cartoon that once again was rather stiff and formal. When the weavers made a mess of it, he sent them a second cartoon, higher and more vivid in tone. It was simpler,

RIGHT:
Sketch of the view from Matisse's hotel window in Tahiti, 1930. Pen and ink, 9⅞ x 12⅝ (25 x 32 cm).

BELOW:
Tapestry cartoons for *Window in Tahiti*, 1936. Each: tempera on paper, 93¾ x 72¾" (238 x 185 cm). Musée Matisse, Nice.

stronger, less descriptive, but it never got woven. Perhaps he wasn't ready to work with his memories of Tahiti.

It took Matisse almost twenty years to distill and simplify and finalize his impressions of Tahiti. But they were worth waiting for.

In the cut-paper images in the 1944 *Jazz* (pages 103, 104), the most daring of all his books, the Tahiti material raised to the surface of his consciousness a precious cargo of aquatic life. There were seabirds, seaweeds, coral, fish, clouds, and the lagoon itself. The forms danced, the color sang out.

There was the velvety Tahitian blue, a blue he had never seen before and could never have imagined. White sails cut into it, marine plants were carried along on it.

The Sails, 1952. Gouache on paper cutout, 28 ⅜ x 23 ⅝" (72 x 60 cm). Private collection.

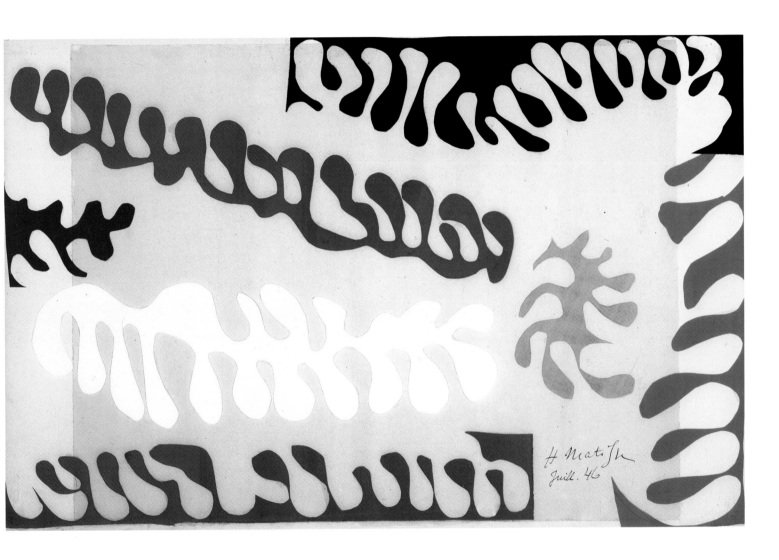

The Lagoon from *Jazz*, 1944. Paper
cutout, 16 x 23 ¾" (40.5 x 60 cm).
Musée National d'Art Moderne, Centre
Georges Pompidou, Paris.

Amphitrite, 1947. Paper cutout,
33 ⅝ x 27 ⅝" (85.5 x 70 cm). Private
collection.

Diving with his eyes open, he had swum for hours in that lagoon. And now his remembered swimmer was half man, half fish, and his marine forms floated free.

Nothing was described in these memories of Tahiti, but everything was there. In fact, Matisse said in the 1950s that what he had brought back from Tahiti was everything that had come later—the Vence chapel, the stained-glass windows, and the great series of big cut-paper compositions.

In that respect, Matisse was the complete traveler. He made Tahiti work for him, just as he had made Nice work for him from 1916 on, and Collioure in 1914, and Morocco in the winters of 1911–12 and 1912–13, and Moscow for a moment in the fall of 1911, and Spain in 1910–11, and Munich in the summer of 1910, and Saint Tropez in 1904, and Corsica in 1898.

But then, Matisse made everywhere work for him, even if it was terrible at the time, as it was when he went to Berlin in the winter of 1908–09 for an exhibition that was a total failure. He was always going

The Swimmer in the Aquarium (reproduced in *Jazz*), c. 1944. Gouache on paper cutouts. 16⅝ x 25 ¾" (42.2 x 65.5 cm). Private collection.

Matisse in Paris, 1949. Photo: Hélène Adant/Rapho.

somewhere, whether on the map of the world or within himself, and something always came of it. But he always moved on.

"To arrive is to be in prison," he once said. I've never forgotten that. And it's true. He never arrived.

But did he ever travel!

Mandolin and Guitar, 1924. Oil and
sand on canvas, 55 ⅜ x 78 ⅞" (140.6 x
200.2 cm). Solomon R. Guggenheim
Museum, New York.

CHAPTER 3

Picasso at First Hand

Photo: Robert Capa/Magnum.

The last thing on earth that most of us want is to have people trooping in to ask favors of us when we have only just got out of bed and aren't even dressed.

But the kings of France put up with that for centuries, and the best composers of the day wrote music for the occasion. People tootled on the flute, scraped on the fiddle, and banged on the drum, while the visitors bowed low and tried to catch the royal eye. As the royal eye was mostly on the royal buttons, it didn't often work. But it was worth a try—and besides, the neighbors fainted away when they heard about it.

By the time I got to Paris in the late 1940s, that particular ceremony had been dead and gone for more than a hundred and fifty years, but there was a large house on the Left Bank where something very like it survived. People went there by the dozen every morning and hung around, hoping to put their case. Finally, an unforgettable human being walked into the room and shook hands with each of them in turn, in European fashion.

No one ever knew what he would do or say, or even whether he would have finished dressing. In warm weather he often came out in just shorts and sandals. But even to be in the room with him was an adventure.

Few people in our century have had so famous a face. His name, of course, was Pablo Picasso. He was short and stocky and, with reason, rather vain of his square, strong body. There was something massive and

Picasso with *Vogue*, c. 1954. Photo:
Robert Doisneau/Rapho.

almost hypnotic about him—above all, when he looked you straight in
the eye—but he was also a champion deflater who could cut straight
through humbug and hype with just a word or two, not to mention a terrible glance. Here was the man who had been creating great art for
almost fifty years at the time I met him. And there was the demon of mis-
chief who had once painted a head of curly hair on the bald pate of his
friend and compatriot, the composer Manuel de Falla. He never lost that
sense of fun.

When we met, I was writing on the arts in Paris for *Vogue*. To tease
me, one day he doctored a sedate fashion photo from the magazine by
adding a pair of black-stockinged legs doing the cancan.

When I was on my way to see him for the first time, I thought over the
long sequences of work—some of them disconcerting, some of them

simple and direct, some of them exhilarating almost beyond belief, and all of them quite fearless—that he had been producing uninterruptedly since our century began.

As a small boy in Spain he had drawn everything around him. When he went to live in Paris in 1901 he went right on recording what he saw, whether it was a prisoner in the dock or a fast-moving narrative about the imaginary adventures of his friend the poet Max Jacob. He had never wavered, never noodled, never not known what to do next.

I remembered the sweet pathos of the Blue and Rose periods (page 110), nearly half a century before, and the arrival in 1906 of a new monumentality in the human figure (page 111). By 1907 the face that looks out at us from his self-portrait (page 207) was that of a man eaten alive by the will to put all of life and all of art into a painting that would be argued over until the end of time. *Les Demoiselles d'Avignon* (page 112) was that painting, and we are a very long way from having said or heard the last word about it.

In 1909 there followed something drier, quieter, and more objective—the first faceting of landscape. Cutting into space the way a sculptor cuts into marble, Picasso reinvented every roof, every wall, every chimney, and every distant hillside in terms of sharp, shadowed angles and flat slabs that slope away from the viewer (page 113).

And then, in 1912, the knot was drawn tight around the neck of all previous art. There was art before these pictures, and art after them, and no one can confuse the two.

ABOVE:
The Prisoner, 1903. Brush, wash, and India ink on paper, 12½ x 8½" (31.6 x 21.6 cm). Musée Picasso, Paris.

RIGHT:
The Plain and Simple Story of Max Jacob and His Glory, or, Virtue's Reward, 1903. Pen and India ink on paper, 7½ x 11⅛" (19.2 x 28.2 cm). Musée Picasso, Paris.

The Family of Saltimbanques, 1905. Oil on canvas, 83 ¾ x 90 ⅜" (212.8 x 229.6 cm). National Gallery of Art, Washington, D.C.; Chester Dale Collection.

OPPOSITE:
Seated Female Nude with Crossed Legs, 1906. Oil on canvas, 59½ x 39⅜" (151 x 100 cm). National Gallery, Prague.

Factory at Horta de Ebro, 1909. Oil on canvas, 20⅞ x 23½" (53 x 60 cm). State Hermitage Museum, Leningrad.

OPPOSITE:
Les Demoiselles d'Avignon, 1907. Oil on canvas, 96 x 92" (243.9 x 233.7 cm). Collection, The Museum of Modern Art, New York; Acquired through the Lillie P. Bliss Bequest.

It was not that Picasso was destroying the traditional norms of painting. He was taking them apart and feeding them into a blender that he and his friend Georges Braque had devised between them. Into that blender went men and women, pipes and glasses, violins and empty packs of cigarettes. Guitars and mandolins, wing collars and watch chains, matchboxes and bottles of rum—all went through the blender of Cubism and came out in combinations without precedent.

Sometimes his images were a continuation of traditional still life by other methods. Scissors and paste ranked equally with paints and pencils. Bits of wallpaper, clippings from newspapers took on a new life. Color went its own way, and the end result was full of puzzles and puns in which our notions of reality were constantly in danger (page 114).

Picasso could make portraits that were as "lifelike" as any in the his-

Apollinaire, 1916. Pencil, 19¼ x 12" (48.9 x 30.5 cm). Private collection.

OPPOSITE:
Glass and Bottle of Suze, 1912. Pasted paper, gouache, and charcoal, 25 ¾ x 19 ¾" (65.4 x 50.2 cm). Washington University Gallery of Art, St. Louis; University Purchase, Kende Sale Fund, 1946.

tory of European art. The great lyric poet Guillaume Apollinaire had been a close friend and fellow gadabout when both of them were young, and Picasso had made many a jokey caricature of him. But when Apollinaire was badly wounded in World War I, Picasso for once drew him in all seriousness. Dignity, simplicity, and straightforward affection were the marks of the portrait that resulted.

But Picasso's deeper instinct during World War I was to dismantle the human body and portray it in terms of flat overlapping planes, often spotted and speckled in ways not found at any tailor's known to me.

In 1916 he made a painting of a man before a fireplace. Once you've cracked the code, this painting presents no problems, but I have to tell

Man Before a Fireplace, 1916. Oil on canvas, 50⅜ x 31⅞" (128 x 81 cm). Musée Picasso, Paris.

The American Manager, from *Parade* (1979 reconstruction after the original of 1917, realized by Kermit Love for the Museum of Modern Art). Tempera on cardboard, wood, fabric, paper, metal, and leather, 134¼ x 96 x 44½" (341 x 243.8 x 113 cm). Collection, The Museum of Modern Art, New York.

you that there was a time when some people mistook it for a view of Manhattan.

In 1917, Picasso got a whole new charge out of Serge Diaghilev's Russian ballet company, for which he made sets and costumes that are as much a part of art history as of theatrical history. For the ballet *Parade* he invented ten-foot-tall characters that functioned like moving scenery. They are not unlike the Cubist figures in his paintings of that period, who might have stepped out of their frames to totter around the stage. One was called the "American Manager"; his costume was made up of skyscrapers, cowboy boots, and a megaphone.

Picasso also got a new wife—his first—out of the Russian ballet: Olga Koklova, a minor member of the company.

Nude Woman in a Red Armchair, 1932. Oil on canvas, 51⅛ x 38¼" (130 x 97 cm). Tate Gallery, London.

As for the traditional subjects of painting—the still life, the studio interior, the female nude—Picasso never strayed from them for long. Yet he made them over in ways that sometimes startled and sometimes reassured, but in either case ended up looking natural and inevitable.

He could paint a still life, all ripe curves, which is a concealed portrait of a new love. And he could portray the interior of the studio in terms of a duel between painter and sitter.

He could take the female nude and work with it over the entire gamut of human experience, from paroxysmal desire to murderous hatred. In *Nude Woman in a Red Armchair*, the brush slithers all over the naked figure in a veritable frenzy of possessiveness, whereas in the *Large Nude*

Large Nude in a Red Arm-chair, 1929. Oil on canvas, 76 ¾ x 51 ¼" (195 x 130 cm). Musée Picasso, Paris.

in a Red Armchair we feel that Picasso would like to take the woman in question, kill her, and gut her. He could be Romeo and Bluebeard, Prince Charming and Jack the Ripper, and into all four of these roles he threw his whole self, without reserve or abatement.

This was the man for whom people came to the big house in the rue des Grands-Augustins—a narrow street on the Left Bank—year after year. It was a large, handsome, seventeenth-century mansion, but at that time it was sufficiently ramshackle to appeal to Picasso, who didn't favor

Rue des Grands-Augustins, Paris.

impeccable settings. (I was amused to see, when I went back recently, that the courtyard had been whitewashed and planted with geraniums. He would have hated that.)

Oddly enough, it was in this very house that Balzac had set the action of *Le Chef d'Œuvre Inconnu*, his novel about a painter. Picasso had made illustrations for that novel in the late 1920s, long before he was to live in the house. The subject suited him particularly: "the painter and his model" was a recurrent theme in his art.

At first Picasso used the house just as a studio, but he moved there in the autumn of 1940, when the Germans were already in Paris, and he stayed all through the Occupation, although he had many invitations from the United States and elsewhere.

It was my neighborhood, too; the office of *L'Œil,* the art magazine I founded, was just around the corner. I used to walk through the big gate, cross the cobblestoned courtyard, turn right, and grope my way up the narrow, leg-breaking spiral staircase to the second floor by the light of a single bulb, which went on for only a few seconds at a time after I had pressed that devilish French invention, the *minuterie* button.

The first time I went to Picasso's, in the spring of 1947, it was because someone had offered to introduce me to him. I had been warned not to wear a hat and not to ask any questions. I followed my instructions and was properly inconspicuous.

At the top of the stairs was a hand-lettered sign: "ICI" (Here). I knocked. The door was opened reluctantly by a parchment-pale, sharp-nosed apparition, who peered at me through thick spectacles. It was

RIGHT:
Jaime Sabartés as a Decadent Poet, 1899. Oil on canvas. Museu Picasso, Barcelona.

FAR RIGHT:
Jaime Sabartés as an Hidalgo, 1939. Museu Picasso, Barcelona.

LEFT:
Kazbec in Picasso's studio in the rue des Grands-Augustins, 1944. Photo: Brassaï.

RIGHT:
Accumulation of cigarette boxes in Picasso's studio in the rue La Boétie, 1932. Photo: Brassaï.

Jaime Sabartés, Picasso's boyhood friend from Barcelona. He had come to Paris, at Picasso's urgent request, in the 1930s, as companion, watchdog, and secretary, and he had devoted his life to treading gingerly in Picasso's shadow, adoring him, and complaining every step of the way. Picasso teased him without mercy, but he couldn't possibly have done without him.

Picasso loved to paint his friends, and he invented the most unexpected identities for them. Over the years Sabartés turns up as a decadent poet, a monk, a horned faun, and a myopic Spanish hidalgo.

Sabartés led me through a small antechamber and into a barnlike studio, where ancient beams held up the high ceiling. There was the big stove that Picasso relied on during the terrible winters of wartime, and there was the astounding accumulation that became part of Picasso's decor wherever he lived and worked. He could never bear to part with anything. Every book, magazine, and catalogue, every piece of wrapping and every last length of string lay where it had fallen, together with every flea-market find, piles of unanswered letters, bits of a broken stove or fragments of sculpture, a stuffed owl, and bulging portfolios of drawings and engravings. If anyone ever left anything behind, there was no hope of getting it back. It stayed on to enrich the loam.

As I was to discover, the line between junk and treasure was very thin. Picasso's incessant compulsion to turn one thing into something else filled what he called his "museum" with such objects as cigar boxes made into miniature theaters with pin-sized actors, and pipe-cleaners turned into jaunty figures. Towers of empty cigarette boxes, glued together, stood waiting their turn for another incarnation. (Until late in life, Picasso smoked incessantly.)

Before overwhelming celebrity made such outings impossible, he liked to go to a bistro just down the street, Le Catalan. Sometimes he would take a pencil and transform the paper tablecloth into a field of fanciful birds and beasts. He molded bread into little figures, and once he took the backbone of a fish he had just finished eating and made it part of an impromptu assemblage.

Like many Spaniards, Picasso lived by night. He liked to work late at night. He never cared about natural light and, in fact, preferred the strong photographic lamps that a former mistress, Dora Maar, who was a photographer, had left behind. If you had the good fortune to have an appointment it would probably be for about noon, when he got up. When I arrived that first time there were, as usual, about a dozen men standing around, waiting. I never saw any women at these noonday receptions. But there were publishers, editors, dealers, poets who hoped for illustrations, unemployed bullfighters.

Picasso finally came in, wearing an old brown dressing gown. The first thing you noticed was the disconcerting intensity of those extraordinary eyes. I understood what Gertrude Stein meant when she said his dark gaze was so intense he could see around corners. I was surprised to see only a light dusting of silvery hair on the well-shaped round head. Photographs from earlier days, with the unmistakable dark forelock (page 159), were so familiar to me that I had not taken account of the passage of time.

Picasso had a ritual greeting, "Please sit down," but there was never any possibility of that. There were sagging sofas and a chair or two, but every one of them was covered with papers, portfolios, dust, and every imaginable kind of dreck. I did a lot of standing at Picasso's.

I was terribly nervous, too, for in spite of his simplicity of manner one was very conscious of being in The Presence. But I was in luck, for I spoke some Spanish, and when he heard his native tongue Picasso lit up with friendly incandescence. He was so passionately attached to his

Picasso at Vallauris, c. 1954. Photo: Karsh, Ottawa.

native country and his native language that from that moment on I felt accepted. He beamed, he asked questions, he stuck around, and before long he began to show me things.

He took me to see the informal arrangements, often balanced precariously, of recent work he liked to show friends. And I was introduced to his Afghan hound, Kazbec. Picasso claimed that Kazbec's elongated snout had found its way into some of his figure paintings of that time.

Then he brought out a book, Aragon's translations from Petrarch, that had a frontispiece by him. He opened it and put it on the floor so that we could take a look. On a blank page at the back, he had drawn a girl's head in colored crayons with five stars across her forehead. It was lovely, and he knew it. "*Très joli,*" he said, in his rolling, Spanish-accented French. (It was my first look at his new love, Françoise Gilot.)

Then with an incredibly mischievous look he went out and got

The Pipes of Pan, 1923. Oil on canvas, 80¾ x 68¾" (205 x 174.5 cm). Musée Picasso, Paris.

another book: poems by Tristan Tzara with black-and-white pen-and-ink illustrations by Matisse. Picasso had colored all the illustrations. Sometimes the color followed the drawing. Sometimes it destroyed it, riding across the lines like a bucking bronco, creating a completely new entity. He knew that I was seeing Matisse. He shot me a glance. "Matisse doesn't know what I've done," said Picasso. (Incidentally, this fascinating document has totally disappeared.)

Not long after that visit, I heard rumors that Picasso was working in Antibes in an old fort, and that no one was allowed in. Naturally there was great curiosity everywhere about what he was doing. I knew that Antibes had served him well before; in 1923 he painted *The Pipes of Pan* there—one of the most majestic of his figure paintings—and the locale had also served for the 1939 *Night Fishing at Antibes*, now in the collection of the Museum of Modern Art.

Just then, he came back to Paris, so I went to see him. There was the usual noonday cast, and Picasso made the usual round. After a while he came over to me and said, "You're the only one here who hasn't asked for something—what would you like?" Seizing the opportunity (one had to jump fast with Picasso when he was in a good mood, and shut up when he wasn't), I said I longed to know what he was up to in Antibes.

To my astonishment, he said, "Why not come down and see for yourself? You have all my benedictions."

So down I went to Antibes and got a look at the outside of the medieval fort, the Château Grimaldi, that dominates the harbor and then guarded the secret of Picasso's new activities. And thanks to his unpredictable generosity, I was the first person from the outside world to see what he had done there and publish it. But it wasn't easy.

Picasso had rented very ordinary rooms right over the main highway to Cannes—he never gave a hang about decor or his surroundings—and he took his meals at Chez Marcel, a café across the street, which is where we were to meet.

I went there. After a while, Picasso came down the road, strong and very brown, in white shorts, red-and-white striped T-shirt, and sandals. I could tell right away that he was in a bad mood. An American dealer had been to his Paris studio, and by mistake Sabartés had let him buy a picture that Picasso didn't want to part with.

I knew better, in that climate, than even to mention my seeing the new work. Picasso would simply have said no to me, as he often did to others. Meanwhile, he was very polite, but he acted as if he had no idea why I was there. The only thing to do was to ride it out.

OPPOSITE:
Picasso in the Grimaldi fortress, 1952.
Photo: Robert Capa/Magnum.

He was a Mediterranean by birth and by temperament. He loved the sun, the beach, and the sea. He had been born by the sea, in Málaga, and had grown up by the sea, in Barcelona. And when he lived in France he invariably—except in wartime—spent summers by the sea: Dinard, Biarritz, the Côte d'Azur. Once Paris was liberated, in 1944, he couldn't wait to get back to the south of France. And he couldn't wait to get away with his new love, the beautiful twenty-three-year-old Françoise Gilot. But he had no house of his own, no place to work except those crowded rented rooms.

At this point, Dor de la Souchère, a local teacher of Latin and Greek who doubled as curator of the Grimaldi fortress, had a brilliant idea. The fortress had been a somewhat halfhearted regional museum before the war, with a scattering of Greco-Roman remains, dolls wearing Provençal costumes, and Napoleonic souvenirs, but it had not reopened. There were splendid empty spaces at the top; why not offer them as a studio to Picasso? If he agreed to work there, there would always be the hope he might leave something behind.

The plan could not have had a greater success. Picasso loved the improvised studio, with the light glinting off the sea and bouncing off the red-tiled floor. He closed himself in. Nobody was admitted except Françoise and his pet owl. Every day his meals were brought in and heated on a little burner while he went to work in a holiday mood.

And in the end he did, indeed, "leave something behind." It is to this day one of the great attractions of Antibes. The old Grimaldi fortress later became the Musée Picasso, Antibes. But I wasn't able to storm that fort for an agonizing week. Picasso specialized in such trials.

The day after my arrival he invited me to join him at the public beach. The group consisted of Françoise Gilot, two Barcelona nephews, his thirty-year-old son, Paulo (whose main interest was high-powered American motorcycles), Picasso's great friend the poet Paul Eluard, and a few hangers-on. And, although they had been separated for years, his first wife, Olga, would come stumbling along, too. Nothing stopped her. Françoise referred to her as "my mother-in-law."

We would swim, eat bouillabaisse at 200 old francs a plate at either Chez Toutou or Chez Nounou, and hunt for interestingly shaped stones on the beach. Competition was fierce for these, with Picasso intent on the chase. Once he picked up a pebble, looked at it, and said, "Oh, we know that one. I saw it last year!" And he threw it back.

Walking on the beach, I was astonished at the amount of gossip Picasso knew: just who was sleeping with whom, who was leaving

Picasso and Françoise Gilot on the
beach at Antibes, 1951. Photo: Robert
Capa/Magnum.

whom. When I mentioned this to Eluard, he said, "But of course, it's
very simple: everybody tells him. You can hardly expect people to talk to
Picasso about art!"

It's hard to imagine today, but at that time the beach was practically
empty. Picasso used it as his office—giving appointments there, holding
court. It was easy to spot the supplicants from Paris—publishers, dealers,
collectors—by their city-white skin. I think Picasso rather enjoyed their
discomfort as they tried to shield themselves from the scorching Midi
sun, holding up their shirts like tents, while he was brown and triumphant.

All this went on for about a week. It was entertaining but nerve-
wracking. Picasso knew very well why I was there, but I knew I should
not be the first to say anything. Finally, casually, as though he had just

thought about it, he asked, "Shall we go and see the paintings? Although bathing is so much more fun. . . ."

The tone of that summer in Antibes was set by a big painting of the year before called *Joie de Vivre*—the title was a bow to Matisse's *Bonheur de Vivre* (page 71), painted many years earlier. It was the work of someone who was in love (the central figure with flowing hair and round breasts is Françoise), and in the south of France, and having a wonderful time after a very grim war.

At that time, there was no canvas to be had in Antibes, and no proper paints. Picasso didn't care. Before the necessary supplies arrived from Paris, he improvised—as he always loved to do. This is a port, he said; they must have good marine paint, and that paint is meant for wood. So he got composition board and housepainter's brushes and went to work.

Antibes had originally been settled by the Greeks, who called it Antipolis. Picasso dreamed up a mythical population of early settlers: pipe-playing fauns, gamboling centaurs, and well-endowed mermaids. In their honor, and to mark his intention, he wrote "Antipolis" on most of these paintings and drawings. "It's a funny thing," he once said. "I never see fauns and centaurs in Paris. They all seem to live around here."

Joie de Vivre, 1946. Oil on composition board, 47¼ x 98¼" (18.6 x 38.7 cm). Musée Picasso, Antibes.

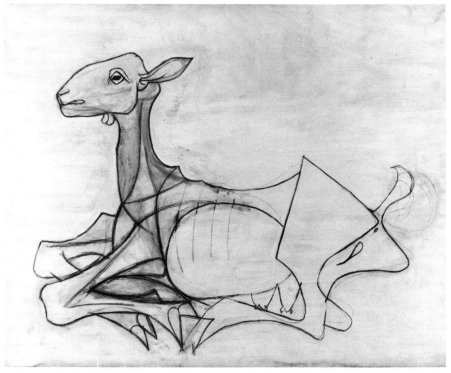

ABOVE:
Still Life with Watermelon, 1946. Oil
and crayon on composition board,
37 ³⁄₈ x 68 ⁷⁄₈" (95 x 175 cm). Musée
Picasso, Antibes.

RIGHT:
Goat, 1946. Oil and enamel, 47 ¹⁄₄ x 59"
(120 x 150 cm). Musée Picasso,
Antibes.

Three Figures, c. 1946. Oil and enamel on a panel of fibro-cement, 98 ⅜ x 141 ¾" (250 x 360 cm). Musée Picasso, Antibes.

It was a world without shadows.

Picasso's Antibes pioneers included his pet goat, Esmeralda. Picasso was always surrounded by pets, and this particular goat was a favorite at the time and followed her master everywhere.

Picasso recorded whatever was around him. Someone must have brought him a watermelon while he was working in his Antibes attic studio, and so it found its place among the fauns and centaurs.

At the time of my first visit to the fort, there were twelve paintings lined up on the floor, none of them signed, along with a few Greco-Roman urns and ratty old plaster casts of Michelangelo's *Bound Slaves* and other sculptures. Were the paintings finished? I asked. Picasso smiled and said, "As long as there is a picture around and I'm anywhere near, it's in danger."

Picasso's habit was to cram the place where he was working to the bursting point, turn the key, and move out. In and around Paris he had a number of studios, each of them full of work, not to mention a honey-comb of bank vaults. But the Château Grimaldi was not his property. Finally, after considerable, if discreet, prodding, he agreed that the works were to stay where they were.

As collectors, dealers, and museum directors knew well, Picasso hated to make up his mind about the disposal of his work. In fact, he didn't like to make up his mind about anything. In the days when he was still based in Paris, the annual summer migration to the south of France was fraught with high drama. The date was set, postponed, changed at the last moment, canceled—all to the despair of his entourage. Finally, on

Lola, the Artist's Sister, 1899. Crayon on paper, 13 ¼ x 9" (33.8 x 23 cm). Museu Picasso, Barcelona.

Menu of Els Quatre Gats, 1899. Printed, 8 ⅝ x 6½" (22 x 16.5 cm). Museu Picasso, Barcelona.

the spur of the moment, everyone and everything got piled ino the old Hispano-Suiza, and off they went. Picasso complained every inch of the way. It was a mistake to have left. He hadn't wanted to go in the first place. But beneath it all, he couldn't wait to get there.

While Picasso did, in the end, give the work done in the Château Grimaldi to the town of Antibes, he made certain conditions. He had strong feelings about whatever he had done in a particular place at a particular time. No matter how oddly assorted the work might look to others, he wanted it to stay together. For this reason he insisted that the still lifes and other unrelated subjects that he had produced in Antibes be shown alongside his jaunty mythological cast of characters.

With Picasso one learned to expect the unexpected. But I was quite overwhelmed when he sent for me in 1954 and said that he had *un regalo*, a present, for me. I was working on the first issues of *L'Œil*, and Picasso suggested that I go to see his sister Lola in Barcelona. He was asking her to show me all the early works by him that had been in her keeping for many years—almost fifty—so that I could write about them. As far as I could tell, no one else from Paris had seen them, and certainly no one had ever published them. And I was apparently one of the first Paris friends to be sent to the family.

All Picasso asked in return was that I tell him all about the trip when I came back. Not only had he not seen his family since 1936, but he had vowed that he would never return to Spain while it was under Franco's rule. He had never even seen his family's present apartment.

Obviously, the idea of seeing unknown work by Picasso was thrilling, and a spectacular boost for the new magazine. I hurried off to Barcelona.

It was in Barcelona that Picasso first became a part of a cosmopolitan, artistic milieu. Barcelona had poets. It had magazines. It had collectors. It had an artists' café: Els Quatre Gats—"The Four Cats" in Catalan. When he was eighteen Picasso designed a menu for it, and he had his first exhibition there that same year—portrait sketches of his friends, tacked up on the wall.

I knew that Picasso's sister, Señora de Vilató, the widow of the director of the Barcelona Psychiatric Clinic, was elderly and in very frail health. So I was rather surprised when I telephoned for an appointment, on arriving in Barcelona, to hear an excited voice say, "Oh yes, we've been expecting you. Come on over. Come at eleven tonight." That was a somewhat unusual hour to visit a sick old lady, I thought.

The Vilatós lived at 48 paseo de Grácia, which is a street of prosperous-looking apartment houses and expensive shops. The well-maintained building and the smoothly running elevator were in great contrast to Picasso's chaotic and crowded quarters and ramshackle staircase. Once inside the front door, however, I realized that the collective family personality was too much for any bourgeois conventionality.

The door was opened. I was ushered into a little hall. I heard voices saying, "We're so pleased to see you."And I said I was so pleased to see them, but in fact I couldn't see a thing. I was plunged in total darkness. The voices were saying, "It's the fuses. They go, they blow like that, *por nada.*" And then they steered me, since I couldn't see my way, into another room.

When I got used to the dark—one part of one lamp was functioning—I made out a round, heavy form seated in an armchair, rising out of a cocoon of blankets. It was Doña Lola, and I could guess that she had once been a great beauty. This was confirmed later, when I saw the sketch that Picasso had made of her in 1899. When Picasso saw the photograph of her that we published in *L'Œil,* he said, "Isn't she splendid! She looks like a bullfighter's mother!"

LEFT:

Lola, the Artist's Sister, 1899. Oil on canvas. Museu Picasso, Barcelona.

RIGHT:

Doña Lola, 1954. Photo: Inge Morath/Magnum.

The Vilató family, 1954. Photo: Inge
Morath/Magnum.

I joined the family: a daughter, Lolita, and two sons, Jaime and Pablín.
We sat in a circle in formal Spanish fashion, wedged between the walls
and an old upright piano, and we made conversation. I brought the Paris
news. They politely asked for mine. They thought it very dashing that a
young woman had come all by herself from Paris to Barcelona. It hadn't
occurred to any of them, ever, to go to Paris. They were obviously
devoted to Pablo, but they seemed to have absolutely no idea of his great
celebrity.

They explained to me that Doña Lola had very severe rheumatism; it
was painful for her to dress or move around. And so she stayed bundled

First Communion, 1895–96. Oil on
canvas, 65 ⅜ x 46½" (166 x 118 cm).
Museu Picasso, Barcelona.

up. But there was no question of hushed voices around the invalid in that
family. One and all, they seemed to live by night. They sat Doña Lola up
in a chair, and then they sang, played the guitar, danced flamenco around
her, and everyone drank little glasses of sweet Málaga wine as the hours
flew by.

In a photograph of the family, one can dimly make out a large painting on the back wall. Doña Lola explained to me that the subject was
suggested by their father, Don José. The painting is Picasso's *First Communion*. Don José posed for the standing figure on the left and she, Lola,
posed for the kneeling girl. She said she hadn't wanted to pose. She

didn't have a first communion dress, but Pablo had insisted and Pablo was used to getting his way. So she borrowed a dress from a friend and did what he wanted. Pablo was fourteen years old at the time.

When I arrived I had given Lolita the big bunch of flowers I'd brought, blue agapanthus. She disappeared with them, and then came back with string still tied around the stalks. The flowers were plunked into the coal scuttle and stuck out at an odd angle. "That's the way it is around here, not like anywhere else," she said. She was right.

As they chatted, elements of the family picture began to emerge. Doña María, Picasso's mother, was very much like him, they told me—short, dark, vivacious. She believed in him implicitly. After he had gone off to Paris she wrote to him at one point: "Now I hear that you are writing poetry. I'm willing to believe it. If I hear next you're saying Mass, I'll believe that, too." However, his father—an unsuccessful painter of dining room pictures who specialized in fur and feathers—was absolutely Pablo's opposite in every way. Tall, thin, fair, he had a very difficult time making a living; Pablo often recorded his care-worn face. His friends called him "el inglés"—the Englishman. Picasso was fifteen when he painted his parents' portraits.

LEFT:
Portrait of the Artist's Mother, 1896. Pastel on paper, 19⅝ x 15⅜" (49.8 x 39 cm). Museu Picasso, Barcelona.

RIGHT:
Portrait of José Ruiz Blasco, the Artist's Father, 1896. Watercolor on paper, 10⅛ x 7" (25.5 x 17.8 cm). Museu Picasso, Barcelona.

Father with Small Drawings, c. 1899.
Crayon and pen on paper, 15⅞ x 12⅝"
(40.2 x 32.1 cm). Museu Picasso,
Barcelona.

The family talked to me about someone Picasso had described as "a
very boring old aunt, a religious maniac who was constantly telling her
beads." This was Tía Pepa. They had wanted a portrait of her for some
time, but the old lady had always refused to pose.

And then, one scorching summer day when Picasso was back in
Málaga for the holidays, she suddenly changed her mind and showed
up—despite the heat—in cap and shawl. Young Pablo, the family
Polaroid, was out playing with his cousins. He was called in. He took out
his paints and brushes. He went to work.

He liked to claim that he had finished the portrait in an hour (page
138), but he was not above exaggeration in such matters. He also said,
with some satisfaction, that she died the following week.

I could easily understand, from all of their high spirits, how Picasso as

Tía Pepa, c. 1895–96. Oil on canvas, 22⅝ x 19⅞" (57.7 x 50.5 cm). Museu Picasso, Barcelona.

a very young man in Barcelona must have had a palpable vibration of energy and well-being. He was beautiful and he knew it. He was a master of the rapid sketch from life, whether it was his sister ladling out the soup or himself trying out the effect of a white wig—he always loved disguises.

The Vilatós told me about another large painting hanging in the apartment, *Science and Charity*. Don José had thought that if his teenaged son painted something with an edifying subject, it would make a good impression in academic circles. And so he staged the scenario and once again posed, this time as a doctor taking the pulse of an unfortunate woman dying in bed. She is comforted by the ministrations of the Church in the person of a nun.

Picasso's personal taste ran to friskier subjects, however, and from first youth until the day of his death he had a strain of wild, freewheeling impropriety.

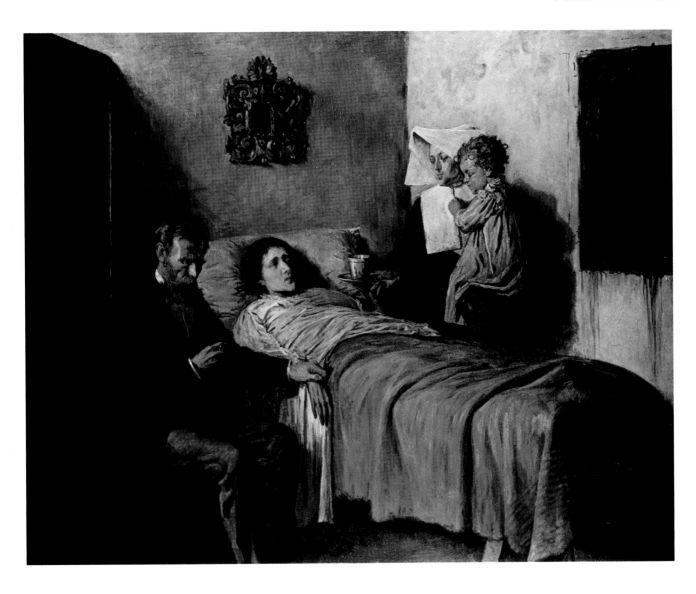

ABOVE:
Science and Charity, 1897. Oil on canvas, 77 ⅝ x 98 ¼" (197 x 249.5 cm). Museu Picasso, Barcelona.

RIGHT:
Erotic Scenes, 1902. Brush and India ink on paper, 8 x 12 ¼" (20.4 x 31.2 cm). Musée Picasso, Paris.

Incidentally, everything I saw at the Vilatós' was black with grime. But many years later, *Science and Charity* and all the other works that were at 48 paseo de Grácia were given to the Museu Picasso in Barcelona, where they were cleaned and restored.

When I was giving up all hope of seeing the rest of the pictures—it was well past one in the morning—Doña Lola finally said, "Oh, maybe she'd like to see the other paintings." So I was gently propelled through more darkened rooms, avoiding a high-backed sofa, massive pieces of Spanish furniture, and what seemed to be glass-fronted bookcases. There were pictures all over the place—on the floor, against the furniture, on the sofa, hanging askew from a single nail. All of them unframed, and all of them dim with the dust of decades.

Lolita, who was escorting me, said, "You can't see very much, can you?" And then she obligingly began lighting matches and holding them up to the pictures. It wasn't very satisfactory. So I asked her, "Couldn't I come back by daylight?" Daylight! That threw them into a state of consternation. They went over their schedules. Nobody was up in the morning. And then they had breakfast. I could hardly believe what I knew to be true: that both Pablín and Jaime were doctors and received their patients at this apartment. I really wondered what sort of office hours they kept.

They thought it over and said, well, it was all right, I could come back the next day, but not before six in the evening. So at six o'clock the next evening I was back, and it was then that I discovered that aside from the early work there was a whole cache of paintings that Picasso had made in 1917 and left in Barcelona after he designed the ballet *Parade*. He became involved with this ballet because the poet Jean Cocteau, who was a great persuader, persuaded Picasso, who loathed travel, to join Serge Diaghilev and the Ballets Russes company in Rome, and do the sets and costumes. The music was to be by Erik Satie, and the choreography by the very young Léonide Massine, a protégé of Diaghilev who got his chance when Nijinsky left the company. When the troupe moved on to Barcelona, Picasso followed them. This was not because he was crazy about the ballet—in fact, he told me that it bored him; what he liked were little circuses and music halls. However, as we've seen, he had fallen in love with one of the dancers, Olga Koklova.

As a proper Spaniard, Picasso didn't take his mistress home. They stayed at a hotel by the port, the Rancini (it doesn't exist anymore), and he worked there. Being Picasso, in spite of being in love, in spite of being involved with the ballet, he did paintings that have nothing to do with

View from Hotel Window, 1917. Oil on canvas. Museu Picasso, Barcelona.

OVERLEAF, LEFT:
Person with Fruitbowl, 1917. Oil on canvas, 39⅜ x 27⅝" (100 x 70.2 cm). Museu Picasso, Barcelona.

OVERLEAF, RIGHT:
Seated Woman, 1917. Oil on canvas, 45⅝ x 35⅛" (116 x 89.2 cm). Museu Picasso, Barcelona.

the dance, and curiously little to do with what he had been painting in Paris. When it was time to leave, he just couldn't be bothered to pack up all that he had done, so instead of shipping the paintings to Paris, he left them with his family, and they had been in Barcelona gathering dust ever since.

Among the 1917 crop was a figure built up in typical Cubist flat overlapping planes, but with the surprising addition of a hand in *trompe l'œil* that seems to be bursting through the canvas (page 142). I had mistakenly thought it represented a seated diner with a compotier of fruit (which is how the Museu Picasso has labeled it), but when I showed a photograph of it to Picasso, he corrected me: "No, it's a waiter setting the table. Can't you see he is holding a knife and fork in the same hand?"

There was another 1917 painting (page 143) that he simply called *Figure* (although the Museu Picasso calls it *Seated Woman*). It was totally unlike anything I had seen from that period. The "figure," with its full

Woman with Mantilla, 1917. Oil on canvas, 45 ⅝ x 35 ⅛" (116 x 89.2 cm). Museu Picasso, Barcelona.

OPPOSITE:
Blanquita Suárez, 1917. Oil on canvas, 28 ⅞ x 18 ½" (73.3 x 47 cm). Museu Picasso, Barcelona.

curves, had connotations of both human anatomy and musical instruments. It was painted in broad surfaces of chalky tones—a dusty pink, almond green, gray, white, black—and painted so thinly that the bare canvas can be seen in several places. This was uncharacteristic of him. When I talked to Picasso about it in Paris, he agreed that it was "*hors série,*" as he put it—one of a kind. It represented, he said, certain preoccupations that he was to take up later.

There were also two paintings of Spanish dancers in the 1917 series. What is fascinating is that although they are very different, Picasso claimed they were painted within a few days of each other. Picasso would veer rapidly from one style to another. One painting had a straightforward frontal approach, the features modeled, the upper part

of the figure and its surrounding space highlighted by a confetti hail of colored dots. The other dances to a Cubist tune, in colors reminiscent of Juan Gris—slate gray, brown, dull green. Departing from the usual immobility of Cubist figures, an elongated arm holding a fan suggests a swirl of movement.

When I returned to Paris I asked Picasso whether the seated dancer was a portrait of Olga, as the Vilatós had told me, and he said, "Absolutely not. That's a totally different painting they are thinking of." He added, "I can't quite remember this dancer's real name because we always called her 'La Salchichona' "—The Sausage.

Another picture in the Vilató house spoke for Picasso's delight in the passing moment. He had painted the view from the hotel room where he lived with Olga: the Christopher Columbus column, a suggestion of masts in the harbor, and the dazzling Catalan sky just touched in with multicolored brushstrokes (page 141). The painting is now used as a poster for the Museu Picasso.

I had also discovered, when I got back to 48 paseo de Grácia in the daylight, that what I had thought were bookcases were indeed that, but instead of books they were filled with plaster casts of deformed feet. That was Dr. Pablín's specialty. When I reported this to Picasso he was delighted, being himself no mean hand at deforming limbs.

Obviously I had a lot to talk over with Picasso when I got back to Paris.

Things could change quite fast around him. When I went to the atelier to tell him about my Barcelona visit, Françoise Gilot was gone and Jacqueline Roque, who was to become his second wife, had moved in. Her love and her looks were to be indispensable to him for the rest of his life. So when I came to report on the Barcelona family, she was called in to hear the news.

As promised, I showed him photographs of the apartment. He looked attentively at the furnishings and exclaimed, "Hah! They live better than I do." When he spied the 1904 engraving called *The Frugal Repast* in a photograph, he said, rather sharply, "I didn't remember they had that. It's worth a fortune now." And then he saw a photograph of a Madonna-like bust and said, "Isn't it ghastly? I've always loved it. It's a *collage avant la lettre*"—a collage before collage existed. He explained that his father had made it. He'd bought a bust of Venus in the flea market, then draped it with cloth dipped in plaster. He painted the face as realistically as possible, added eyebrows and golden tears, and made it Our Lady of Sorrows.

Our Lady of Sorrows made by Picasso's father. Photo: Inge Morath/Magnum.

The same photograph shows a picture on the wall—a drawing of Picasso's father that Picasso made when he was fourteen. One corner of the glass is broken and another drawing is stuck in the frame. That's about how everything was in the apartment.

Picasso loved presents, and he lost no time in opening the ones I had been entrusted to bring back to him. I knew that the heavy boxes contained *membrillo*—a sweet gelatinous substance that only a Spanish palate can appreciate. Next came a penny bank in the form of a rooster. It rattled: the family had put a coin in for good luck. Then there was a paper bag stamped with the name of a pork butcher. It was full of sugared almonds. "That's Spain for you," Picasso said. "You buy candy at the butcher's."

Next came a carefully wrapped package with a lot of tissue paper. Rolled up inside it was a handful of cotton seeds. Picasso looked around his studio with its heaped canvases, its books, its antediluvian papers, its portfolios, magazines, and sculptures and said happily, "They're just what we need. Let's plant them right here."

It would have been difficult to go to Picasso's studio at any time during the seventy or so years of his career and not get a sense of who was in or out of his life. The women in question were there, in the work, not only as sitters or as objects, but as barometers and weather vanes. Sometimes the weather they signaled was paradisal. Sometimes it made the visitor reach for his umbrella, his long johns, and the train schedule, the quicker to leave town.

When I first got to know Picasso, the person still most often thought of in this context was Dora Maar, although the two had separated some years earlier. When Picasso first knew Dora, in the late 1930s, she was a handsome young woman with striking dark eyes and a strong jaw. She was of Yugoslav descent and had grown up in Argentina, and she spoke Spanish—a big plus with Picasso. Unlike some of her predecessors in his affections, she was intelligent and well educated, and had gifts and ambitions of her own. Over the years, her face was to play many roles in his work, from the radiant serenity of someone who knows that she is loved to the extremes of anguish and loss.

At first, Picasso drew and painted her in tenderness and wonderment.

Dora Sleeping, c. 1935

Picasso and Dora Maar at Golfe-Juan, 1937. Photo: Roland Penrose.

But nothing could withstand his will to reinvent, and before long her features were yanked from their normal alignment, pushed into simultaneous profile and full face, and reassembled in ways to which the pressure of external events had contributed.

As a comment on the Spanish Civil War, Picasso's huge mural *Guernica* would be hard to equal. Dora Maar was with Picasso throughout the six weeks in 1937 that it took him to complete it, and she made a photographic record of its progress that is invaluable to the historian. And among the single-figure postscripts to *Guernica* that he painted not long after, the most powerful—known as *Weeping Woman*—is, in effect, a portrait of Dora Maar (page 151).

As always with Picasso, an unmistakable personal likeness of the model remained, no matter how savage the distortions. I first met Dora Maar in a crowded restaurant in Paris, where introductions were drowned out by the din. I found myself looking across the table at a woman whom I seemed to know, although I had never met her before. And then I recognized her. Of course! It was Dora Maar.

She once took me to see a portrait that Picasso had painted of her in the same fateful year as *Guernica*. We went deep into the vault of the Crédit Lyonnais in Paris, where she kept it. She and Picasso had parted, long since, in a way that had left her deeply disturbed. But the painting that came out of the vault was of Dora on a beach in high summer, with

Portrait of Dora Maar, 1937. Oil on canvas. Collection Dora Maar, Paris.

her head resting on her crossed arms. It was so fresh that one could almost feel the sea breezes blowing.

Dora had found Picasso his studio in the rue des Grands-Augustins and she herself took a small apartment in the rue de Savoie nearby. As my office was in the next street I often used to go and visit her there. By the time I met her she was working seriously on painting, and I noticed that her white walls were sprinkled with small painted beetles and butterflies. She said they had begun as tiny splashes of paint that she had flicked off her brushes as she worked. One day Picasso came by and transformed every speck of paint into a little insect.

It was in the same room that in 1943 Picasso brought her the very first copy of the edition of Buffon's *Histoire Naturelle* that he had illustrated. As he could never leave anything alone, he sat down at once and began to embellish the book with drawing after drawing in ink. Down the margins, all over any empty page, birds, beasts, and mythological heroes came to life. As frontispiece, he drew Dora herself as a radiant bird.

Picasso showed his lifelong love of puns by inscribing the book to her with the author's name changed to "buffoon," in relation to himself, while "A Dora" was turned into "J'adore Dora."

Dora was not, by the way, an uncritical admirer of Picasso. When we went together to see *Le Mystère Picasso*, the film by Henri-Georges Clouzot, I felt in her a combination of real emotion and exasperation. Naturally it was fascinating for me to watch Picasso at work in the film, but when he came out with one of his favorite sayings—"You shouldn't

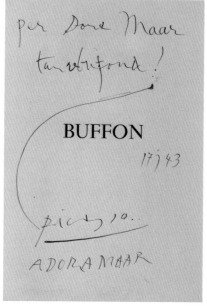

Pages of Buffon's *Histoire Naturelle* inscribed by Picasso, 1943. Collection Dora Maar, Paris.

Weeping Woman, 1937. Oil on canvas,
23⅞ x 19¾" (60.8 x 50 cm). Tate
Gallery, London.

OPPOSITE:
The January 1955 issue of *L'Œil*, signed by Picasso, Georges Braque, and Daniel-Henry Kahnweiler.

look for truth at the bottom of a well"—she groaned, "Oh my Lord! If you knew how often I had to hear that old chestnut!"

While Picasso's black moods could be annihilating, his kindnesses to me were memorable. Once he sent me a photograph of himself reading *L'Œil*, with Jacqueline Roque looking over his shoulder. What a wonderful thing it would be, I thought, if he would allow us to use it to publicize the art review. I wrote, asking his permission. Writing to Picasso was like sending a message in a bottle—he never answered. But I thought I should at least try.

He didn't answer with a letter, but by return mail I received a strip of Leica negatives with shot after shot of Picasso with my magazine. "L'œil" means "the eye," and in one striking image—unfortunately, I don't own it—he was holding up the cover of the magazine with its title right under *his* eye. We used that picture, with the line, "Do as He does,

Picasso and Jacqueline Roque reading *L'Œil*, 1957.

Du temps que les cubistes étaient jeunes

UN ENTRETIEN AU MAGNÉTOPHONE AVEC DANIEL-HENRY KAHNWEILER

Kahnweiler vendait la peinture cubiste quand on ne l'achetait pas. Il en vend encore aujourd'hui. C'est dire qu'il est un de ceux qui connaissent le mieux la petite et la grande histoire de l'art contemporain.

Bernier./ De 1902, date de votre arrivée de Francfort à Paris, à 1907 où vous avez ouvert votre galerie, avez-vous fréquenté les milieux artistiques ?

Kahnweiler./ *Non, pas du tout, c'est beaucoup plus drôle que cela. Je suis arrivé à Paris parce que mes parents, qui étaient dans des affaires de finance, m'y avaient envoyé, chez un agent de change. On ne voyait pas d'autre avenir pour un rejeton de la famille qu'un avenir de financier. J'allais à la Bourse chaque jour quelques instants pour me faire voir de mon patron, puis je fichais le camp au Louvre. J'ai continué ce manège pendant deux ans et demi ; ensuite, en 1905, mes parents m'envoyèrent à Londres, où étaient installés mes deux oncles, l'un d'eux surtout, Sigmund Neuman, Sir Sigmund Neuman Baronet ensuite, un des fondateurs des mines d'or d'Afrique du Sud. Comme à Paris, je faisais de mon mieux pour en faire le moins possible. En décembre 1906, la famille décida que j'irais à Johannesburg. Je dis alors : « Je ne me sens aucun penchant, vous vous en êtes déjà aperçus, pour le métier de la banque et de la bourse. » — « Mais qu'est-ce que tu veux donc faire ? » — « J'aimerais mieux être marchand de tableaux. » Je n'avais pas vu de peintres à Paris, où je ne connaissais personne, mais j'avais beaucoup fréquenté les expositions et j'avais commencé à me faire une petite collection de gravures, notamment des eaux-fortes de Manet, des lithos de Lautrec et de Cézanne. Mes oncles ne poussèrent pas les hauts cris, ce que mes parents seuls auraient fait à coup sûr. Ils décidèrent de me faire passer une sorte d'examen. Pour cela, ils m'envoyèrent chez Wertheimer, un des plus grands marchands de la ville, qui vendait surtout des tableaux anciens du XVIIIe, des Gainsborough, etc. C'était un très honnête homme et certainement, à sa façon, un excellent marchand. Il me demanda, par exemple : « A la National Gallery, qu'est-ce que vous aimez ? » Je fis exprès de prendre le contrepied de ses goûts. Si je lui avais dit que j'aimais Velasquez — que j'aimais d'ailleurs beaucoup — il aurait trouvé cela magnifique. Je déclarai : « J'aime beaucoup le Greco. » Or le Greco, à ce moment-là, sentait encore le soufre. Je dis aussi que j'aimais beaucoup Vermeer qui, à l'époque, n'était pas très apprécié, et je citai deux ou trois noms de ce genre.*

Puis il me demanda : « Mais enfin, vous comptez ouvrir une galerie ; qu'achèterez-vous donc ? » Je connaissais déjà l'existence de Derain, de Matisse, des fauves en un mot. Je me dis : Si je lui indique ces noms-là, il me répondra : « Connais pas ». Je décidai de citer Bonnard, Vuillard, dont je pensais qu'il avait pu entendre parler. Il me répondit: « Connais pas ».

Néanmoins mes oncles, qui étaient des gens compréhensifs, me firent l'offre suivante : « On va te donner 25.000 francs et un an. Si, à la fin de l'année, tu es arrivé à des résultats, tu continueras ; sinon, tu iras en Afrique du Sud. » Le marché conclu, je partis aussitôt. Nous arrivâmes, ma femme et moi, le 22 février 1907 à Paris. Je trouvai bientôt une boutique rue Vignon. Les Indépendants ouvraient au mois de mars, et je fis là mes premiers achats, qui étaient des choses de Derain, de Vlaminck, de Braque, des fauves enfin.

B./ Qu'est-ce qu'un jeune homme passionné pour les arts plastiques, comme vous, voyait alors de la peinture contemporaine?

K./ *Le Luxembourg, vous le savez, était à l'époque le dépotoir de toutes les gloires de la peinture officielle. Il n'y avait que la toute petite salle Caillebotte où on pouvait voir de la peinture vivante. Dans les salons, on trouvait la peinture de ceux qui se sont groupés, en 1903, pour fonder le Salon d'automne. Il y avait d'une part Matisse (Picasso n'exposait jamais), Braque, Vlaminck, Dufy, Friesz, d'autre part Rouault.*

B./ Cézanne vivait encore. Son œuvre était-elle connue ?

K./ *Il y avait eu, précisément au Salon d'automne en 1904, une grande rétrospective Cézanne. Les Indépendants avaient fait aussi, vers ce temps-là, des rétrospectives de Seurat et de Van Gogh. Ces peintres avaient donc des amateurs qui formaient une petite, mais enthousiaste minorité. Quant à moi, je les admirais, mais il me semblait qu'au point de vue affaires, c'était trop tard.*

B./ Mais pour ne pas parler de Cézanne, de Seurat ou de Van Gogh, les toiles des impressionnistes, déjà plus largement appréciées, paraissaient-elles « lisibles » au grand public ?

K./ *Ah, pas du tout. On était encore très loin même des impressionnistes. En 1904, lors d'une exposition des Monet de Londres chez Durand-Ruel, je me rappelle avoir vu deux cochers de fiacre, convulsés de haine, tendant les poings, qui voulaient démolir la devanture parce qu'ils étaient furieux contre ces tableaux qu'ils ne comprenaient pas.*

B./ En somme, le public, même averti, qui ne savait encore qu'à peine lire l'impressionnisme, et encore bien moins des œuvres comme celles de Seurat, de Cézanne et de Van Gogh, s'est trouvé brusquement mis en présence de la révolution cubiste. Il y eut là une sorte de télescopage.

K./ *En effet, mais pour être tout à fait précis, le public ne s'est pas trouvé confronté*

D.H. Kahnweiler
photographié par Picasso en 1912.

avec le cubisme, puisque les grands peintres de ce mouvement n'ont plus voulu exposer dans les salons parisiens. Picasso n'a jamais participé à ces manifestations ; il avait montré sa peinture une fois chez Vollard en 1901. Braque, lui, avait exposé des

Altered cover and inscribed pages of *El Entierro del Conde de Orgaz*.

open your eye," and nobody in France had to be told who "He" was.

When the first issue of my magazine came out in 1955, it carried an interview with Picasso's old friend and dealer from the early days, Daniel-Henry Kahnweiler, and it included a photograph of Kahnweiler taken by Picasso in 1912. In a routine way I gave Picasso his credit for the picture. He was simply thrilled. He carried this issue of *L'Œil* back to his atelier and showed it to everybody. "*There's* a really intelligent art magazine," he would say. "They know I'm a photographer." My own copy of that number was signed by Picasso, by Georges Braque, with his characteristic palette signature, and by Kahnweiler (page 153).

Some years later Picasso sent me a little book he had written and illustrated himself. It was called *El Entierro del Conde de Orgaz*, after the famous painting by El Greco, and it brought together all kinds of unlikely bedfellows—Velázquez and the great bullfighter Manolete, for instance—and a torrent of images, both verbal and visual, that he took from his own surroundings.

With his usual itch to change everything he touched, Picasso had inscribed it all over the cover, making my name part of a face. He had repeated the inscription inside, possibly from affection for me but more probably because he couldn't bear to leave a blank page alone. He misspelled my name twice, but that did not surprise me; he had a very free-wheeling, eighteenth-century way with spelling. In fact, he once told me that he had never learned the alphabet and had no intention of ever

doing so. "Why should one letter follow another in a predestined order? Ridiculous!"

He carried on his embellishments on another page inside the book, and conjured up a man wearing a squashy hat. He always loved fanciful hats, and one of the happier days of his life was when Gary Cooper came to see him in the south of France and gave him his classic ten-gallon hat. For weeks after that, Picasso insisted on going around in only shorts and that hat. As I've said, he adored disguises of all kinds, the more ridiculous the better, and since people knew that, he was sent things from all over: false noses, false whiskers, funny spectacles. When he was expecting some person of importance who had never seen him before, he liked to get himself up to startle and disconcert the visitor who had been preparing himself for weeks to meet the Master. The unfortunate visitor wouldn't know whether to laugh or to pretend that Picasso always looked like that.

Picasso often painted his portraits from memory, and when he was fond of people he was apt to combine the features of more than one of them on the same canvas. Some of the portraits he painted during the occupation of Paris were composite images in which room was found for both Dora and Nusch, the frail and lovely wife of his friend Paul Eluard. They were not really at all alike, but Picasso filled out Nusch's fragile face to rhyme with Dora's, and he gave Dora's robust good looks something of Nusch's wistful delicacy.

Less tactfully he sometimes combined the features of his mistresses— there are portraits of Marie-Thérèse Walter and of Dora where it is almost impossible to tell which is which. The subjects could hardly have been pleased.

Paul Eluard told me how delighted he and his wife were when Picasso told them that he was going to give them the portrait of Nusch as a present. He meant it, too. But when it came to finding paper and string to wrap it up, he simply couldn't bear to part with them. "No, no, that's really too beautiful," he would say, and put the picture away until their next visit. It took him months to get over the problem.

No one ever had greater powers of metamorphosis than Picasso. He applied them to people and to books, as we have seen, but he also applied them to great works by others. One of these was *The Women of Algiers in Their Apartments* by Eugène Delacroix (page 156), of which Picasso made fifteen variants in the winter of 1954–55.

Already in January 1940, when he was living with Dora in Royan, near Bordeaux, he made drawings after the *Women of Algiers* in a sketch-

LEFT:
Jacqueline in a Turkish Vest, 1955. Oil on canvas, 39⅜ x 31½" (100 x 80 cm). Galerie Beyeler, Basel.

RIGHT
Eugène Delacroix, *The Women of Algiers in Their Apartments*, 1834. Oil on canvas, 71 x 90⅜" (180 x 229 cm). Musée du Louvre, Paris.

OPPOSITE:
The Women of Algiers, after Delacroix.
TOP: Variation N, 1955. Oil on canvas, 44½ x 57⅜" (113 x 145.7 cm). Washington University Gallery of Art, St. Louis, University Purchase, Steinberg Fund, 1960.
BOTTOM: Variation O (final version), 1955. Oil on canvas, 44⅞ x 57½" (114 x 146 cm). Private collection.

book. When he gave some of his finest pictures to the French state in 1946, they were hung for a while in the Louvre, by way of acknowledgment and commemoration, and Picasso was invited to come and see them. It pleased him very much that Delacroix's *Women of Algiers* was hung not far away.

And when, later, he was living in Paris with Françoise Gilot, he used to take her to the Louvre "on average once a month" to look at it. One day, on the way home, he narrowed his eyes and said, "That bastard Delacroix! He's really good." Some day, he said, he would make his own version of the *Women of Algiers*.

That day came in 1954, when his future wife Jacqueline Roque entered his life and he became fascinated by the resemblance between her and the main figure in Delacroix's painting. And Jacqueline really did look very much like her—the same proud nose, the same abundant black hair, and the same well-knit body. When Picasso painted her in Turkish costume the likeness became even more obvious.

According to Picasso's friend and neighbor Hélène Parmelin, the *Women of Algiers* came to dominate the Picasso household during the winter of 1954–55. First place was given, without question, to "colloquy with Delacroix, life in common with Delacroix, the introduction of Delacroix as a guest at mealtimes." Picasso kept wondering, he said, what Delacroix would say if he walked into the studio.

And then he really got down to it.

I went to Picasso's studio in Paris with my friend, Picasso's biographer Roland Penrose, to see the variations (two of which are reproduced on page 157). Even singly, they never fail to captivate, but all together, with the paint still wet on them, they charmed away the discomforts of a particularly bitter Parisian winter. When Picasso brought them out one by one and stacked them around the room, we were dumbfounded by their vigor, their variety, and their sense of purposeful fun.

They were full of echoes, too. When Roland remarked that although Delacroix had been the point of departure, there was much of Matisse in both the Moorish interiors and the provocative poses of the girls, Picasso agreed. "Quite right," he said. "When Matisse died, he left me his odalisques as a legacy."

The fifteen paintings were completed in less than two months. (Two of them were dated on successive days.) From beginning to end, Picasso upped the stakes as he went along. As usually happened when he paraphrased a painting from the past, he took the characters and wrote them a new scenario in paint. Delacroix's thoughtful women of the harem in their hushed interior took on—both literally and figuratively—a new coloration. Loosening their silks and velvets, they flaunted bosoms and buttocks as ripe as watermelons.

On the right of Delacroix's *Women of Algiers* in the Louvre is a seated figure. When Picasso first began to work on her, he put her to sleep, as if sated with pleasure. Then she woke up, stretched out luxuriously on her back, and, in the end, twirled her legs in the air. In this, as in much else, Picasso took what in Delacroix had been shadowy, ambiguous, and languid and made it over in the image of his own explicit and voracious nature.

In the last painting of all (Variation O), Delacroix's subdued interior has become a gaily striped tent. To the left, the towering figure of Jacqueline dominates the scene, as mistress of the revels. Planes of strong color are tilted this way and that, and there is a sense of get-up-and-go that was not at all how Delacroix remembered Algiers.

As Roland Penrose recalled it later, one of Picasso's visitors remarked that the *Women of Algiers* series did not seem to have any one general direction. Picasso agreed, and said that he never knew what was coming next. Nor did he ever try to interpret what he had done. "That's for others to do," he said, "if they feel like it." To make his point even clearer, he brought out a large recent aquatint of his that showed a group of people, some of them old and ridiculous, others young and handsome, watching a painter working at his easel.

"You tell me what it means," he said, "and what that naked old man with his back to us is up to. Everyone who comes here has *his* own story about it.

"I'm the only one who doesn't know what's going on. But then, I never do. If I did, I'd be finished."

And as we all know, Picasso was *never* finished.

Picasso in the late 1930s. Photo: Man Ray.

CHAPTER 4

What Picasso Kept for Himself

N o one danced, that evening in Paris, but everyone had a ball. The great house was lit up as it had not been lit up for two hundred years. Quite possibly it had never looked so handsome, with its sphinxes smiling down on the cobblestones of the courtyard, the stone coat of arms looking squeaky-clean just behind the high roof, and a big striped tent set up in the garden at the back. Even the neighbors were pleased to see the Hôtel Salé brought back to life.

Built in the seventeenth century with new money—and a great deal of it—the Hôtel Salé had lived many lives. Its first owner had had trouble with people who thought that he had made too much money, too fast, and got rather above himself. "Is this the only house you have?" they said, preening themselves on their huge country estates and their fortified Renaissance castles. "It's the only house I need," said the proud first owner, and he didn't ask them over again.

Then the house became successively the Venetian embassy, a center for arts and crafts, a school in which Balzac was one of the pupils, and more recently a kind of derelicts' collective. Every room was cut up into ten, every window was broken many times over, and every inch of available space was occupied, legally or illegally, by metropolitan monkeys who kept one jump ahead of the police.

Eventually the city of Paris bought the Hôtel Salé and saved it from certain destruction. But no one knew quite what to do with it. You could

Violin Construction, 1915. Painted steel, 37½ x 25⅝ x 7½" (94.5 x 65 x 19 cm). Musée Picasso, Paris.

LEFT:
Musée Picasso, Paris. Photo:
Rosamond Bernier.

RIGHT:
Main staircase, Musée Picasso, Paris.
Photo: Rosamond Bernier.

have got long odds at that time against its ever becoming what it is now—the Musée Picasso. Yet there it was, on that fine summer evening in 1985, remade inside and out, and packed with people who had crossed the world to see it. Not only did it look right and feel right, but it was full of things that helped us see Picasso in a new way—and not just the familiar Picasso, either, but a supplementary and, in some respects, an alternative Picasso.

It had been a colossal task. When I originally went there with Dominique Bozo, the founding director of the museum, workmen were everywhere—in the courtyard, in the house, in the garden. Some people thought that the Hôtel Salé was too big and too grand for Picasso. It's Picasso versus Louis XIV, they said, as if that was a battle that Picasso couldn't win.

It was true that the Hôtel Salé was a very handsome house—even the cellars had a lot of style. The main staircase was a triumph of seventeenth-century design, and it had been embellished with sculptures that were rich and full and ample. But when I was there, and Picasso's big

Musée Picasso, Paris: Room 13, cellar.

Women at the Spring was being installed, it looked perfectly at home. So did his *Man with a Lamb*—one of the most famous of his later sculptures—whether it was outside in the courtyard or just inside the door, where it now greets the visitor.

The truth is that Picasso's work had always looked its best in grand spaces. It had also to be borne in mind that in this case there was more of Picasso to deal with than most people would have believed possible.

Characteristically, Picasso had died without leaving a will. No one knew how much he had kept himself or what it was like. Everyone knew of major artists whose leavings had had to be burned, in their own best interests, and of others whose unfinished works had been "completed" and sold. What if that happened again?

It fell to Dominique Bozo and a team of helpers to sift through the mountain of material stashed away in Picasso's various studios, not to mention the mass of paintings in bank vaults that took months to review. By the time he and his team had finished sorting through the estate, Bozo realized that he had to deal with more than 1,200 sculptures and 700 drawings, and at least 23,000 engravings and lithographs—besides the hundreds and hundreds of paintings.

Every possible obstacle had seemed to be in the way of a Picasso museum in Paris that would be worthy of the name. The French had taken forever to get the point of Picasso. He was seventy-three before he had a major museum exhibition in Paris. Before 1914, much of his best

The Infanta Margarita María from *The Maids of Honor (Las Meninas), after Velázquez*, 1957. Oil on canvas, 39⅜ x 32" (100 x 81 cm). Museu Picasso, Barcelona.

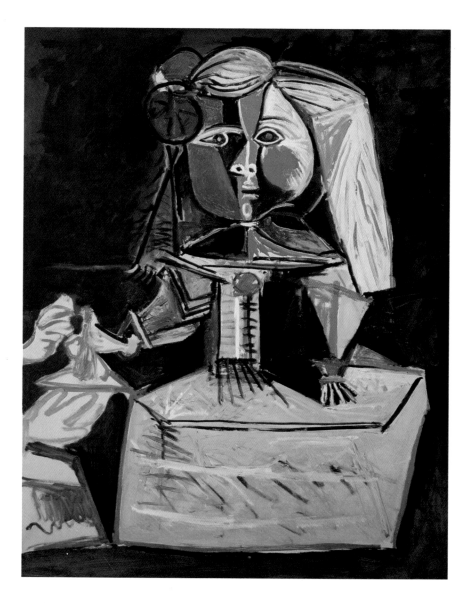

work went to private collectors in Russia. Swiss and Czech collectors were also way ahead of the French. Nor did Alfred Barr and his colleagues at the Museum of Modern Art in New York have to fear competition from the French when they were building their great Picasso collection.

All these were heavy losses to any potential Picasso museum in Paris. But Picasso had no particular reason to think kindly of Parisian museums and, besides, there was already a Picasso museum in a city he loved, Barcelona.

His old friend, confidant, and longtime secretary, Jaime Sabartés, got the idea of the museum in Barcelona going when he gave his extensive Picasso collection—which included a number of portraits of him by Picasso (page 120)—to his native city. After Sabartés died in 1968, at the age of eighty-six, Picasso gave the infant museum the entire series of fifty-eight paintings that he had made after what many people consider to be the greatest picture ever painted by a Spaniard—Velázquez's *Las Meninas*. Picasso made separate studies of the individual figures, shifting them around like a theater director putting a cast through its paces.

Two years later, to everyone's astonishment and delight, Picasso gave the Barcelona museum virtually everything that he had left with his family in Spain. This gift made the Museu Picasso the most substantial repository of the work of his first youth (he was nine when he drew the lively bullfight scene on this page), and of what he had done in Barcelona when he went back for a visit in 1917. These were the paintings and drawings that Picasso's family in Barcelona had shown me, at his request, many years before (pages 141–145).

Picasso's first wife, Olga Koklova, died in January 1955. They had been separated for many years. If he never made a legal break with her, it was because under French law any such break would have entitled her

Bullfight, 1890. Pencil on paper, 5 ⅜ x 8" (13.5 x 20.2 cm). Museu Picasso, Barcelona.

Olga Picasso in an Armchair, 1917. Oil on canvas. 51¼ x 34⅝" (130 x 88 cm). Musée Picasso, Paris.

Bust of a Woman with Self-Portrait, 1929. Oil on canvas, 28 x 23⅞" (71 x 60.5 cm). Private collection.

to half of what was in his studio. For that and other reasons, very few people knew how much he left behind him, intact, when he left a studio that he had crammed to the limit and moved on to another.

In 1917 he painted Olga as the well-born lady she would have liked to be. But he grew to hate her, absolutely and without qualification, and there is more than one painting to prove it. By 1929 he had turned her into a sharp-tongued monster, and to drive home the point he added his own profile to the background. Roland Penrose, who owned this picture, used to tell me that the green stripe indicated that the monster lived on poison.

Olga was vapid and pretentious. Initially Picasso had been rather tickled by the fact that she was the daughter of a White Russian army officer, but in the end her social ambitions bored him. When he was bothered every day with invitations to fancy parties in Paris, he pinned a note on his studio door that said "I am not a gentleman," and waited for the hostesses to get the point.

Picasso and Olga occupied two apartments in the rue La Boétie in Paris. Olga's domain was a conventional living room, peopled in the drawing below by some unconventional guests: besides Olga there are Jean Cocteau, Erik Satie, and the English critic Clive Bell. On the floor above was Pablo's domain—the studio.

With Olga out of the way, it was clear from Picasso's first-ever Parisian museum retrospective in June 1955 (a few months after her death) that all previous estimates of his career would have to be readjusted in the light of what he had kept for himself. Just what he had kept began to emerge in this retrospective exhibition. Above all, it gave a hint of how much he had done in sculpture, and how little of it he had let out.

People knew of early sculptures by Picasso, such as *Blind Man* of 1905, and the 1909 Cubist portrait head of Fernande Olivier. But fundamentally there was just too much of him for people to have taken on any more. No one realized to what extent his career was truly what Dominique Bozo calls a "duet for painting and sculpture."

ABOVE:
The Artist's Studio in the rue La Boétie, 1920. Pencil and charcoal on grey paper, 24⅝ x 18⅞" (62.5 x 48 cm). Musée Picasso, Paris.

RIGHT:
The Artist's Living Room in the rue La Boétie, 1919. Pencil on paper, 19¼ x 24" (49 x 61 cm). Musée Picasso, Paris.

LEFT:
Blind Man, 1905.

RIGHT:
Woman's Head (Fernande Olivier),
1909. Bronze, 16¼ x 9¾ x 10½"
(41.2 x 24.8 x 26.7 cm). Collection,
The Museum of Modern Art, New
York; Purchase.

It came as a revelation to many that, as of 1912, Picasso had invented a completely new kind of sculpture. Neither carved nor modeled, it was *built*, the way a carpenter builds a table or a chair. First he made a gaunt, formal, unadorned statement, in the sheet-metal *Guitar* of 1912, which he kept for almost sixty years, until he gave it to the Museum of Modern Art in New York in his ninetieth year.

But later that same year, 1912, Picasso was building his guitars with mixed materials—in one case (page 171), cardboard, pasted paper, cloth, string, oil, and traces of crayon. This was a guitar that led a life of its own. You couldn't play it. It didn't look like art. No one could say it was well crafted. In fact, the most you could say of the subjects of these sculptures is that they had been set free from their workaday context and touched by a wizard. They had nothing to do with taste, as it is generally understood, but everything to do with the mysterious life of forms and the ways in which that life can survive and flourish in unprecedented circumstances.

Jolie Eva, 1912. Oil on canvas, 25 ⅝ x
31 ⅞ " (60 x 81 cm). Staatsgalerie,
Stuttgart.

Still-Life Construction, 1914. Painted wood with upholstery fringe, 10 x 18 x 3⅝" (25.4 x 45.7 x 9.2 cm). Tate Gallery, London.

Guitar, 1912. Cardboard cutout, pasted string, oil, paper, cloth, crayon, 13 x 64⅛ x 3" (33 x 16.3 x 7.5 cm). Musée Picasso, Paris.

Some of Picasso's sculptures—or constructions, as they are usually called—lived in a kind of no-man's land between painting, sculpture, and home carpentry. They always began with a familiar subject—a glass, a newspaper, a bottle of brand-name English beer—but there was no limit to the ways in which he could present and re-present that subject.

Some of those early constructions were intimately related to Cubist paintings of the same period. As Picasso said to a fellow Spaniard, the sculptor Julio González: "All you had to do with those paintings was take a pair of scissors and cut into them. The colors were no more than indications of differing perspectives or planes inclined this way or that. Once the cutting was done, you just had to put the pieces together as the color indicated, and there in front of you was a sculpture."

We can see what he meant if we look at paintings like *Jolie Eva*, of 1912. They could take to the third dimension the way a crab takes to Chesapeake Bay.

The constructions were *really* duets for painting and sculpture. They were remarkable for their original and radical use of unexpected materials, and for the freedom with which Picasso used the jut and thrust of the third dimension. He didn't care if his constructions looked awkward and unstable. He wanted them to say what he wanted to say. What other people made of them was their own affair.

Untitled engraving, 1968.

We got to know more about the hidden Picasso when his eighty-fifth birthday was marked by a huge exhibition in Paris in 1966. But Picasso did not like to be regarded as a historical monument and, eighty-five or not, he wasn't going to stop working. Between March and October 1968, he produced no fewer than 347 engravings, as if to show that it was too soon to draw a thick black line at the bottom of his dossier.

These engravings show a wild, ribald, free-running fantasy, as if he had reached a time in life at which everything could come out and his hand still knew just where to go. Some of them have echoes that go a long way back, to the great painting of 1905 called *The Family of Saltimbanques* (page 110). Picasso was always haunted by the idea of a group of strolling players who went from town to town in a cart and had every kind of adventure on the way.

If you look hard, you can see Picasso making a cameo appearance as the local photographer in one of these engravings.

Picasso also liked to let his fancy go free among men in historical costume and young women in no costume at all. In every one of these strange encounters that he set before us, there was a sense of wonder, as if he had trouble believing the images that the needle had cut into the plate. But there was also something of the circus manager who had just

Untitled engraving, 1968.

The Kiss, 1969. Oil on canvas, 38⅛ x 51¼" (97 x 130 cm). Musée Picasso, Paris.

landed a whole series of new acts that would fill the tent, day after day.

He went on painting, too, although many people rather wished that he wouldn't. They had him taped and trussed. His every twist and turn had been monitored and made sense of. They knew everything about Picasso. What business had he to come up not simply with a new period but with a whole new idiom?

He had said his say in 1925 about the spectacle of two people kissing as if their lives depended on it. It was really too inconvenient to find that in 1969 he had a whole other set of ideas on the subject. And what ideas, too!

Picasso in the previous sixty or seventy years had painted in a great many ways, but fundamentally he had always painted like someone who was completely in control. In his last years he painted in ways that were loose, and splashy, and approximate. A new Picasso—as poignant as he was ribald—was among us, and many people found that very disconcerting.

What if he had even more secrets to spring, and the whole Picasso industry—for that is what it had become—would have to be restructured? Why must he carry on like an overexcited little boy who refused to go to sleep?

This was the situation when Picasso died in 1973. As we have seen, he left no will, but he left not only a widow, but children and grandchildren, legitimate and illegitimate.

OPPOSITE:
The Kiss, 1925. Oil on canvas, 51¼ x 38⅛" (130 x 97 cm). Musée Picasso, Paris.

A look at the photograph below will suggest the possible complications: Here is Picasso reigning like the king of the Gypsies at a bullfight in Vallauris in 1955. Behind him is Maïa, his illegitimate daughter by Marie-Thérèse Walter, and Claude, his illegitimate son by Françoise Gilot. Next to him is Jacqueline Roque, who would become his second wife, and in the foreground is Paulo, his legitimate son by his first wife, Olga. One of the few people in this photo not related to Picasso is his friend Jean Cocteau, who is on Picasso's left.

With at least seven heirs in prospect, his estate had a potential for chaos that could not be overestimated. If his heirs had not been per-

Picasso with family and friends at a bullfight, 1955. Photo: Brian Brake.

The Children's Tea Party, 1943.

suaded to reach a rational agreement with one another, and with the French government, they would still be in litigation today. It was finally agreed that in lieu of inheritance tax the French government should have first refusal of whatever it needed for a Picasso museum. I may add that there was plenty left over for the heirs to dispose of as they wished.

The estate of Picasso was, in effect, an autobiography that covered much of his life in its every last detail. Everything was there, from the pass that he had had to present every day when he was installing *Guernica* at the Paris Exposition of 1937 to the photographs, many of them taken by Picasso himself, that documented his comings and goings, year by year. There were letters, postcards, memorabilia of every kind. As I mentioned before, Picasso never threw anything away. Had all this been dispersed, it would have been a disaster.

Difficult as it often was to remember it, Picasso had his full share of fatherhood, even if it never lasted very long. An unexpected document that came to light in Picasso's papers is a drawing he made of himself as the complete family man, presiding over a tiny tots' tea party. His more usual preoccupations are sketched on the same sheet: a bullfight scene and a pet goat.

As he never let anything go to waste, Picasso put his experience of

OPPOSITE:
Girl Jumping Rope, 1950. Bronze,
60¼ x 25⅝ x 24⅜" (153 x 65 x
62 cm). Musée Picasso, Paris.

RIGHT:
Photograph of the Bateau-Lavoir,
annotated by Picasso. Musée Picasso,
Paris.

Marie-Thérèse Walter at seventeen,
c. 1927. Musée Picasso, Paris.

family life into sculpture. Like many of his pieces from the 1950s, these sculptures are made up of elements that started out in life with quite different functions and identities. Here is, for instance, the pedigree of the *Girl Jumping Rope*:

To begin with, Picasso had a Vallauris hardware store make a base and a curved iron tube which became the rope. The child's body was made from one of those flat baskets used in the south of France to pick orange blossoms for the perfume industry. He folded some papers and attached pieces of them to the bottom of the basket, making the skirt. These were then cast in plaster. He carved the legs out of wood and added two old shoes found on a dump heap. The face was made from the plaster imprint of a round chocolate box cover. The hair started out as corrugated cardboard.

Also among his personal effects was a photograph of the Bateau-Lavoir, the dilapidated house where Picasso had a studio in the first decade of the century—he painted *Les Demoiselles d'Avignon* there in 1907. The photograph has been annotated by Picasso to show the window of his atelier.

And there were photographs of people or events that by now have mythic stature, and the more so because Picasso's involvement with them was so intense. This is particularly true of Marie-Thérèse Walter, the ripe Germanic-looking young woman Picasso picked up on the street when she was only seventeen. "I am Picasso, and I want to paint you," was his opening gambit, and although she had no idea who

OPPOSITE:
Nude in a Garden [Marie Thérèse Walter], 1934. Oil on canvas, 63 ¾ x 51 ⅛" (162 x 130 cm). Musée Picasso, Paris.

BELOW, LEFT: Marie-Thérèse Walter, photographed by Picasso, c. 1932. Musée Picasso, Paris.
BELOW, RIGHT: *Bather with Beach Ball*, 1932. Oil on canvas, 57 ⅝ x 45 ⅛" (146.2 x 114.6 cm). Collection, The Museum of Modern Art, New York; Partial gift of an anonymous donor and promised gift of Ronald S. Lauder.

Picasso was, she fell for it. If she started out looking like a demure schoolgirl, Picasso soon changed all that.

Is it imaginable that she was as voluptuous as he made her look? His many paintings of her would suggest that yes, she was. She apparently was horizontal a good deal of the time, and often asleep.

His own photographs also indicate that even his wildest images started from everyday fact. Her bulk, her beach ball, her rudimentary haircut—all found their way into the paintings.

This is only one of the many contexts in which the autobiographical material simply had to be kept together. Marie-Thérèse appears again and again in the Musée Picasso, in material that he kept for himself: his own photographs and his many portraits of her, in sculpture and paintings and in combinations of both. There are oblique references to

Bather Opening a Cabin, 1928. Oil on canvas, 12⅞ x 8⅝" (32.8 x 22 cm). Musée Picasso, Paris.

demonic embraces and to the erotic possibilities of a bather opening up her beach hut with a key.

The Musée Picasso was full of surprises. No one had expected the chair-palette that Picasso had turned into a cross between a painting and a sculpture. When I saw it, I remembered that Picasso never used an ordinary palette. Once he was sent a transparent palette—glass or lucite—by a New York dealer, but he didn't like it. At the rue des Grands-Augustins there was a low table covered with thicknesses of newspaper. Picasso used to squeeze paint right onto the table, dip his brushes in turpentine, then wipe them on the newspapers before loading them with paint. When the papers were too clogged, they were thrown away and another layer was put in place.

And there is a majestic and alarming New Hebrides sculpture that came to Picasso as a present from Matisse. By the way, Picasso said that he thought Matisse had given it to him because it was so scary that only he, Picasso, could deal with it.

During the process of searching and researching that went on for several years, it became clear that, quite apart from finished works in this medium or that, the Picasso estate was astonishingly rich in complete sketchbooks. Many of them had obviously never been opened since they were first filled and put away.

Chair and Palette. Musée Picasso, Paris.

In all, 175 sketchbooks were identified. They ranged in date from 1894, when Picasso turned thirteen, to 1967, when he was not far short of ninety. Even in old age he treated every new sketchbook as an event to be celebrated in color.

Picasso looked on his sketchbooks as friends and accomplices. There was one with a message on it. Painted, as much as written, it says: "I am the sketchbook that belongs to Monsieur Picasso, painter, of 13 rue Ravignan, Paris 18." That is where Picasso lived at the beginning of the century.

He also made handwritten notes—addresses, appointments, facts that caught his fancy—that tell us exactly whom he was seeing, and when,

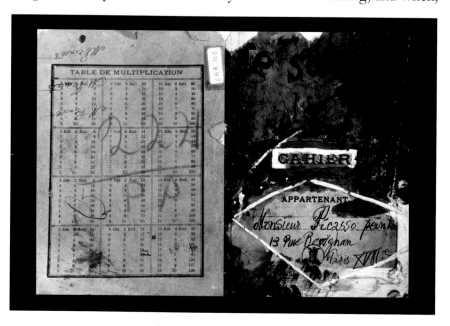

TOP:
Sketchbook cover, 1906.

BOTTOM:
Sketchbook 138, 1956–57.

Drawing related to *Les Desmoiselles d'Avignon*, Sketchbook 42, pages I and J, 1907. Ink on paper, 6½ x 4⅜" (16.5 x 11 cm).

although not always why: "Braque Friday; Thursday 12:00 at Foyot Restaurant."

Picasso never edited his sketchbooks. Page by page, almost without exception, they were as he had left them. Even the most important ones—those relating, for instance, to *Les Demoiselles d'Avignon*—had not been opened for many years.

Scholars who had lived in hopes of finding new evidence about that great and daunting picture were amazed to find that historical documents of the very first order had been folded like credit-card receipts and tucked into a cheap imitation leather wallet. Even when he could have

Sketchbook 35, 1905. Pencil and
watercolor on paper, 5 ⅝ x 3 ½"
(14.5 x 9 cm).

afforded fancy papers and Florentine bindings, Picasso went on using
ten-cent notebooks.

It would take weeks to go through every one of those sketchbooks. It
would take years to elucidate them completely. Besides, you have to
know what you are looking at. You have to know that the strong, busty
drawing of a cabaret singer is related to Picasso's first visit to Paris in
1901. He drew her, however implausibly, in a sketchpad from England
that was called "The Public Schools Drawing Book."

Then there is a sketch of a hefty old veteran. It relates to a figure in the
Family of Saltimbanques. By contrast, the drawing of the little girl was
clearly done from life, just because Picasso happened to spot her in the
street. He never lost an opportunity, no matter how intent he was on a
grand design.

There was a time when people didn't want to think of Picasso as a colorist. The idea was that he was at his very best in the early and high
Cubist periods, when color was virtually banished from painting. But in
the notebooks there are some tiny sketches made in 1915, measuring no
more than a few inches in either direction. They function as chromatic
possibilities that simply block in the outline of an eventual picture. But
they are the work of a virtuoso colorist. A painting of the same year,
Man with a Pipe, makes the point on a grand scale.

This is one of the most gorgeous pictures Picasso ever painted. It is a
riot of detail, with buttons enough for a tailor's dummy, hands strong
enough for any chairman of the board, a big derby hat of the kind current at the time, and the lowered eyes and elegant eyebrows that Picasso
must have lifted from a famous painting by Giorgio de Chirico. No one

RIGHT:
Sketchbook 57, 1915. Each: pencil, ink,
pastel, and/or watercolor on paper,
6 ¼ x 5 ½" (16 x 14 cm).

OPPOSITE:
Man with a Pipe, 1915. Oil on canvas,
51 ¼ x 35 ¼" (130.2 x 89.5 cm). Art
Institute of Chicago; Gift of Mr. and
Mrs. Leigh B. Block in memory of
Albert D. Lasker.

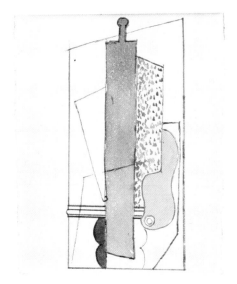

LEFT:
Sketchbook 77, p. 5, c. 1922. Pencil on paper, 16½ x 12" (42 x 30.5 cm).

RIGHT:
Sketchbook 76, p. 37, 1922. Pencil, watercolor, and/or pastel on paper, 6⅛ x 4½" (15.5 x 11.5 cm).

could possibly have inferred that Picasso put this delicious painting together at a time when his dearest friends could have been killed at any moment.

When World War I began, Picasso was moved to the extent of writing *"Vive la France!"* on a separate sheet and folding it inside his current sketchbook. He never failed to note the military numbers and addresses of his French friends who had gone to the war. But where his work was concerned, the war was off limits.

Picasso had perfect scale, the way some musicians have perfect pitch, and I don't think anyone would imagine that his monumental presentations of cloudless motherhood are actually very small. Nor does it seem likely that the little boy in question, who looks as if he were made out of sugared almonds, would grow up to care for nothing but the heaviest and fastest thing in motorbikes. But he did.

In the days when Picasso rented a new house each summer, at his wife's insistence, he liked to make precise drawings as soon as he moved in. In fact, he turned round and round like a dog in a new basket. He got the outside of the house, he got the inside of the house, and he got all

The interior of Villa Beauregard (Dinard), from Sketchbook 77, p. 5, c. 1922. 12 x 16½" (30.5 x 42 cm).

kinds of unexpected details, as if he wanted to be in complete control of his new environment.

Just such drawings were made in Dinard, in Brittany, in 1922. Later, Dinard came to have a special association for Picasso, in that he had stashed away his young mistress Marie-Thérèse there, while continuing to live with Olga, who by then was a terrible burden to him. Even the bathing huts in Dinard were dear to him—probably because he was able to have his way with Marie-Thérèse in one of them under the sad cold nose of his wife.

At the very end of a sketchbook he used in Dinard there is a seraphic image (page 190) that appears to have walked in from another time and another life. But it may also be two things in one. It is certainly a still life of particularly delicious fruit, but it is also—or so I think—a coded memory of Marie-Thérèse's fullness and roundness and readiness to be bitten into.

Sketchbook 99, 1929. Pencil and
brown pastel on paper, 1 1 ¾ x 14 ¾"
(30 x 37.5 cm).

The Swimmer, 1929. Oil on canvas,
51 ¼ x 63 ⅜" (130.2 x 161 cm). Musée
Picasso, Paris.

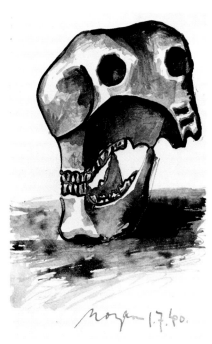

Sketchbook 110, inside front cover and p. 28, 1940. Each: ink on paper, 9⅝ x 6¼" (24.5 x 16 cm).

Picasso is said to have boasted that unlike most men he could make love under water. It may or may not be relevant to this controversial matter that, as far as I know, he never learned to swim. He loved to splash around, but that was as far as it went. Yet he knew all about the ecstatic contortions that swimmers can get into—Marie-Thérèse was very athletic (page 191).

Then there came a time when everything spoiled, all over Europe. Picasso and Dora Maar, who succeeded Marie-Thérèse as his mistress, were living in Royan at the end of May 1940. The Germans had already crossed the border into France, but when Picasso began a new notebook on May 31, he could still turn his hand to an untroubled, hedonistic nude.

But by August 1, even Picasso had to take a grim view of the future. The human head turned into a fleshless, eyeless apparition, half skull, half German helmet. Thereafter, deeply but indirectly, the war was present in his work. "I did not paint the war," he said later, "because I'm not that kind of painter. But posterity may decide that the war is there, all the same."

After the war was over, some of his favorite painters from the past made brief appearances in the sketchbooks. In fact there was a day in June 1954 when he penciled in both Edouard Manet, with figures from his *Déjeuner sur l'herbe*, and Eugène Delacroix.

These sketchbooks make up a kind of parallel Picasso, and those of 1962 are very important to our idea of Picasso in old age.

He had just turned eighty-one when he decided to match himself against two of his great predecessors, Nicolas Poussin and Jacques-Louis David, by tackling one of the classic subjects of Old Master painting, the rape of the Sabine women by the soldiers of Rome. He got color slides of the Poussin and the David and projected them on a white wall at home. They made a tremendous effect. It was the time of the Cuban missile crisis, and war was on everyone's mind. Besides, the idea of men taking women by force induced in Picasso a combination of rage, pity, and animal excitement that made his imagination boil over.

To me, Picasso's sketchbook studies for *The Rape of the Sabines* (pages 194, 195) have the reckless assurance of a much younger man, together with the definitive awareness that comes with great age of what can still be done in art. Picasso worked at the sketches hard and fast—on one day he made no fewer than fourteen complete drawings—and there seem to have been no failures among them. The drawings of women's heads are as powerful as anything he ever did, *Guernica* not excepted. Some of the Sabines don't seem to be having too bad a time when the Roman soldiers

TOP:
Nicolas Poussin, *The Rape of the Sabines*, c. 1683. Oil on canvas, 61 x 82½" (159 x 206 cm). Musée du Louvre, Paris.

BOTTOM:
Jacques-Louis David, *The Rape of the Sabines*, 1799. Oil on canvas, 152 x 204¾" (386.1 x 520.1 cm). Musée du Louvre, Paris.

finally get to them. Maybe Picasso was momentarily carried away by the idea of a kind of dormitory romp.

He also worked very hard on the military details, even though he cared nothing for historical accuracy, and at the architectural background, even if that, too, had its slapdash aspects.

For that matter, neither Poussin nor David was a stickler for archaeo-

26.10.62. V

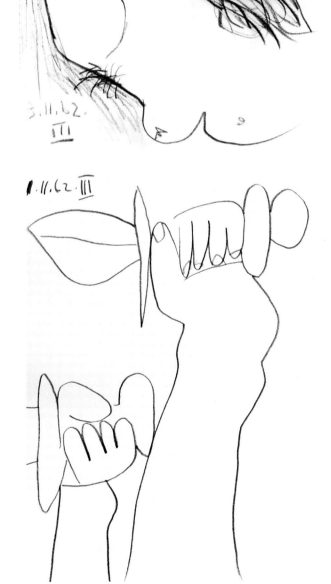

Four studies for *The Rape of the Sabines* from sketchbook 162, 1962. Each: crayon on paper, 10⅝ x 8¼" (27 x 21 cm).

The Rape of the Sabines, 1962. Oil on
canvas, 38 ¼ x 51 ¼" (97 x 130 cm).
Musée National d'Art Moderne, Centre
Georges Pompidou, Paris.

OPPOSITE:
The Rape of the Sabines, 1963. Oil on
canvas, 76 ⅞ x 51 ⅝" (195.4 x 131 cm).
Museum of Fine Arts, Boston; Juliana
Cheney Edwards Collection, Tompkins
Collection, and Fanny P. Mason Fund
in Memory of Alice Thevin.

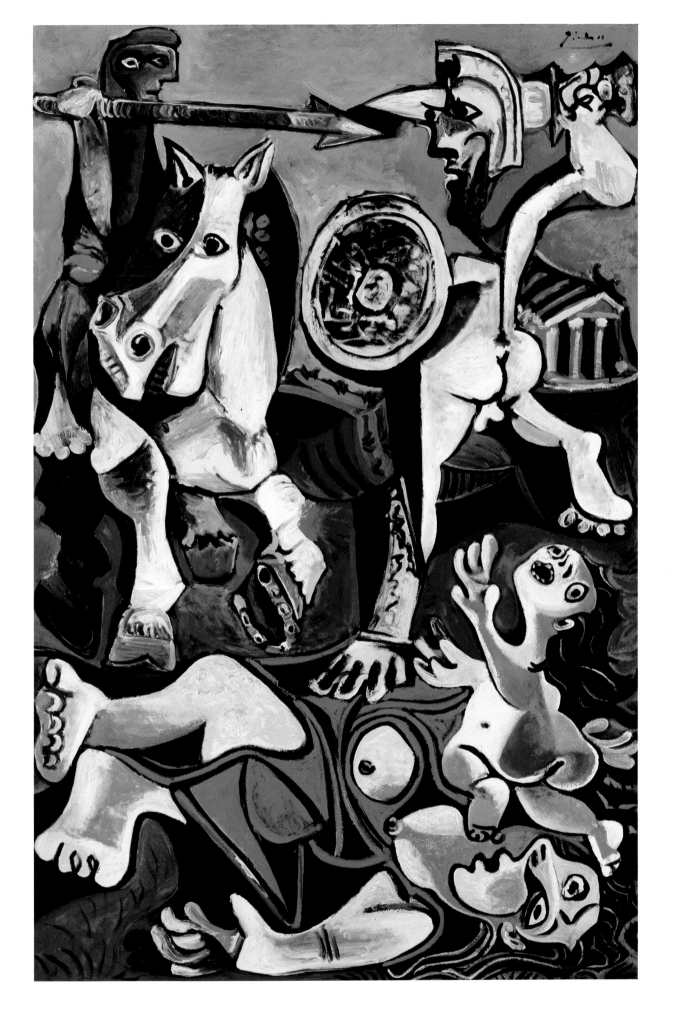

logical accuracy. What they prized above all was expressive grouping, the collective thrust of figures in violent action and the detail that bites home. Poussin in particular was a master of the grand design, but he also knew when to focus on an individual whose most terrible moment this was.

On two successive days, Picasso drafted compositions that had something of both Poussin and David and yet were unmistakably his own.

When Picasso made the two very different paintings for which the drawings were the preliminaries (pages 196, 197), he discarded both the beauty of outline and the occasional incongruous playfulness of the sketches. He went all out for the ugliness, the confusion, and the all-pervading brutality and inhumanity that we know so well from the television news. These were images, slowed and weighted by paint, in which people kill for killing's sake, without distinction of age or sex.

Picasso had many selves, and one of them was alert to everything that had ever been done in art. "Every painter is a collector," he used to say to me. "He collects the images of others, he makes them his own, and he turns them into something quite different. That's real col-

Matthias Grünewald, Crucifixion panel from the Isenheim Altarpiece, c. 1515. Oil on wood. Musée d'Unterlinden, Colmar, France.

lecting. You must take what you can wherever you can find it, except in your own work. I have a horror of copying myself."

One of the more unexpected paintings that he collected, in this sense, was Matthias Grünewald's Isenheim Altarpiece in Colmar. Picasso had already painted a small *Crucifixion* of his own in 1930, and very curious, poignant, and personal it was. But in 1932 he began a series of drawings inspired directly by Grünewald. As always, he went about it in his own thoroughgoing style. In one of the drawings, the gaunt northern statement of Grünewald has been transformed into a kind of irritable bone-

Crucifixion, after Grünewald, 1932. India ink, each: 13 ⅜ x 20⅛" (34 x 51 cm). Musée Picasso, Paris.

yard. In others, he reached a balance between his passion for reinvention and Grünewald's dark fancies.

I once had a firsthand experience of Picasso's way with the northern Old Masters. I had just come back from Munich, where I had been deeply impressed by the paintings of Albrecht Altdorfer, a contemporary of Dürer and Grünewald, in the Alte Pinakothek. Picasso may have hated to travel, but he knew the world's museums by heart through reproductions. "Oh yes," he said, "I've got a book about Altdorfer here." Someone had made the mistake of dropping by the studio with the book under his arm and Picasso, curious as a monkey, had grabbed it and never let it go.

"I even made some drawings after Altdorfer," he said, "of St. Sebastian." The idea of publishing these unknown drawings in *L'Œil* was a heady one to me, and I begged him to let me see them. "How do you expect me to find anything here?" he said with an eloquent gesture at the chaos of his studio. I didn't press the point.

"It would be easier for me to do them over again," he said. "You know, it has happened more than once that someone has called to fetch a drawing that I had promised him and, although it was done, I couldn't find it. So to put things right I would go out of the room 'to look for it,' and while I was away I would do another one just like it. They never knew the difference."

I never expected to see those drawings, but a few days later Sabartés called me and said, "*He* wants to see you." (He never called Picasso by his name.) Naturally I was over in no time. There was Picasso, his work trousers held up by a piece of rope, with a big smile—pleased with himself, and pleased for me. "I found them," he said, "and here they are."

He had made drawings of the whole composition and also studies from details of the painting, and he had signed them "Albrecht Altdorfer" in Gothic letters. I believe they have never been reproduced except

St. Sebastian, after Altdorfer, details.

in my magazine, and in fact I don't think Picasso ever found them again. They don't seem to have shown up in the inventories of his estate.

Picasso was never a collector in any of the accepted senses. He bought what he had to have, for reasons all his own, and he never got rid of it. His personal art collection is now part of the Musée Picasso in Paris.

He was known to have a Cézanne *Bathers* of the late 1870s, and a late Cézanne landscape of the Château Noir, near Aix-en-Provence. He had paintings by people he admired, such as the Douanier Rousseau. He loved Rousseau's work, and the man himself, and he had been host at the famous banquet that was held for Rousseau in 1908 in the Bateau-Lavoir, to celebrate the purchase of a large painting of a standing woman. Picasso had bought the painting in 1907—for five francs—and he said it was one of the pictures he treasured most. It was in the place of honor in his studio in 1908, and was draped with a garland and flags for the banquet. The guest of honor played the violin and sang his repertoire of popular songs, including his favorite, *"Aie, aie, aie, J'ai Mal aux Dents."* The painting was still in Picasso's studio in the rue des Grands-Augustins when I first visited him there.

Henri Rousseau, *Portrait of a Standing Woman*, date unknown. Oil on canvas, 63 x 39½" (160 x 105 cm). Musée Picasso, Paris.

Picasso also had two early paintings by Joan Miró, a 1919 self-portrait and the *Spanish Dancer* of 1921 (page 229). Anyone can see why, as a fellow Spaniard and a Catalan by adoption, Picasso had to have them near him.

Needless to say, he had paintings—seven—by Matisse, his rival, his equal, and in a strange, persistent way, his friend. During World War II, Picasso had bought the great 1913 still life of a bowl of oranges on a tablecloth patterned with anemones (page 27).

The two men exchanged paintings on several occasions. Back in 1907, Picasso had traded a still life of his own for an early portrait of Matisse's daughter, Marguerite (page 27). And, as I said earlier, I remember seeing a 1940s Picasso landscape over Matisse's fireplace in Vence.

In another exchange during the 1940s, Picasso chose two of the apparently hedonistic canvases which Matisse had painted during the German occupation of France. Picasso admired the perfect harmony of the colors, and their spontaneity, finding them *"très Matisse."* In return Matisse chose an austere Picasso still life and a head of Dora Maar as *"très Picasso."* Each artist selected what he felt to be characteristic of the other.

Henri Rousseau, *The Representatives of Foreign Powers Coming to Hail the Republic as a Token of Peace*, 1907. Oil on canvas. Musée Picasso, Paris.

There is one major purchase we can easily understand, and that is the series of monotypes by Degas that Picasso bought toward the end of his life. Almost without exception, they are brothel scenes (page 204). Picasso had a lifelong interest in material of this sort, and in his last great etchings he returned to it repeatedly.

More than once, Degas himself appears in those etchings as a tall, impassive, all-seeing presence. In his imagination, Picasso was a voyeur, a witness, a nonparticipant in the antics that had once been the subject matter of perhaps the most influential of all his paintings, *Les Demoiselles d'Avignon.*

Not long ago, the American art historian Robert Rosenblum came across an entry in Picasso's notebooks that suggested that already in 1907, the year he painted the *Demoiselles,* Picasso had heard about these

OPPOSITE, TOP:
Edgar Degas, *The Madam's Birthday*, 1878–79. Pastel over monotype, 10½ x 11⅝" (26.5 x 29.5 cm). Musée Picasso, Paris.

OPPOSITE, BOTTOM:
Sketchbook 42, p. K, 1907. Ink on paper, 4⅜ x 6½" (11 x 16.5 cm).

monotypes by Degas and was interested in seeing them. If that is true, it proves once again that in his collecting, as in everything else he did, Picasso never acted at random.

In life, as in his art, Picasso had a multiple identity, as the following pages demonstrate. No sooner did he portray himself in his Blue Period as a bearded night wanderer, bundled up against the cold, than he started in 1906 to look like an antique marble sculpture that had opted for everyday life (page 206). In 1907, he looked like a man burning at the stake in the fires of his own imagination (page 207). But in 1917, exploring ancient ruins in Italy with the dancer and choreographer Léonide

Self-Portrait, 1901. Oil on canvas, 31½ x 23⅝" (80 x 60 cm). Musée Picasso, Paris.

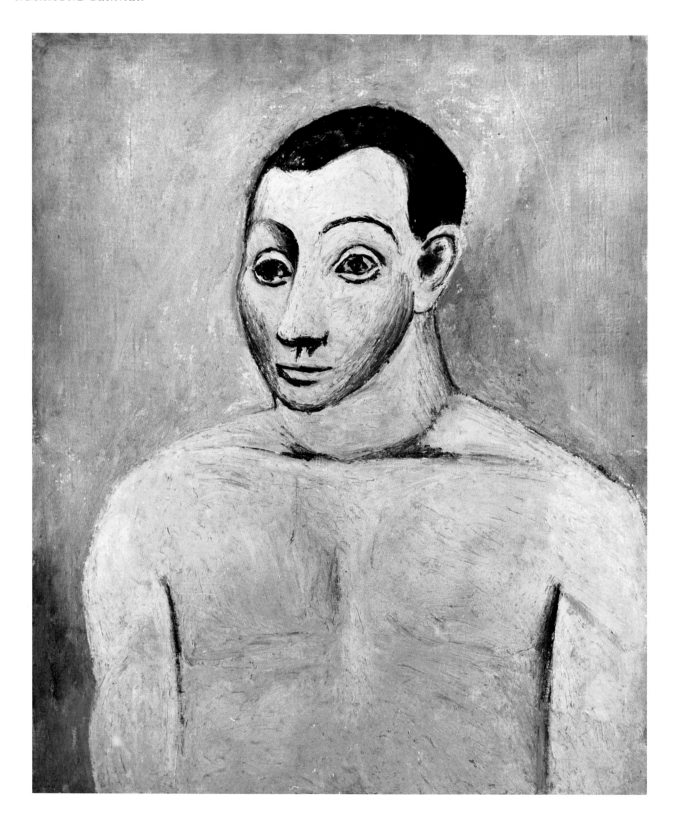

Self-Portrait, 1906. Oil on canvas,
25 ⅝ x 21 ¼" (65 x 54 cm). Musée
Picasso, Paris.

Self-Portrait, 1907. Oil on canvas,
19 ¾ x 18 ⅛" (50 x 46 cm). National
Gallery, Prague.

RIGHT:
Picasso at Pompei, 1917.

BELOW, LEFT:
Self-Portrait, 1931. Sketchbook 101,
p. 32.

BELOW, RIGHT:
Picasso in 1955. Photo: Henri Lartigue.

OPPOSITE:
Self-Portrait as a Skull, 1972. Crayon
on paper, 25 ½ x 20" (65.7 x 50.5 cm).
Fuji Television Gallery, Tokyo.

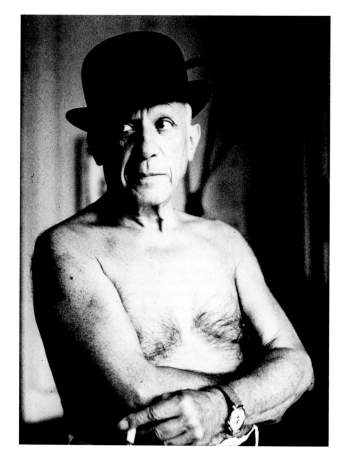

Picasso on the beach at Antibes, 1923.
Musée Picasso, Paris.

Massine, he was every inch the classic sightseer, complete with dark suit, collar and tie, and a cane to help him over rough ground (page 208).

In 1931, just pushing fifty, he was back among us as an aging poet, hardly marked by life (page 208). If we agree with George Orwell that at fifty every man has the face he deserves, then I think we have to say that Picasso was doing well.

He still had more than forty years to live. For almost all of them, he could tell old age to go away and not come back. (Sometimes an ancient bowler hat from Lock's, the famous London hatter, made the message doubly clear.) But when Picasso was ninety, and death was near at last, he looked it straight in the face, without flinching. The skull self-portrait (page 209) is from 1971. I do not know of a more courageous image.

But I prefer to remember Picasso as he was in the prime of life, with his two strong legs planted firmly on the earth, looking rather as Neptune would look if he had decided to step up the beach for a bowl of bouillabaisse. Many years later, in his villa above Cannes, he instinctively took the same proud pose, looking this time like a great captain, with his troops in line of battle behind him, who has nothing to fear from the future.

OPPOSITE:
Picasso at La Californie, 1956. Photo:
Arnold Newman.

CHAPTER 5

Miró at First Hand

"Wear a crown of eyes around your head," said the teacher at the art school in Barcelona. The short, round-faced young man did just that—and he never took it off. His name, Miró, means "he looked" in Spanish. And if you drop the accent on the *o*, as people often do outside of Spain, it turns into "Miro"—"I look." What better name for this painter whose candid blue gaze was to record every last detail of his Catalan environment and the vast reaches of the stars?

This most reserved and silent of artists was born in Barcelona in 1893, but it was the countryside near Tarragona, where his family bought a farm when he was a boy, that never failed to nourish his art. "The smallest thing in nature is an entire world," he used to say. "I find my themes in the fields and on the beach. Pieces of anchors, starfish, shells—they all turn up in my paintings, and so do the preposterous heads of mushrooms and the seventy-seven shapes of the calabash."

Words and parts of words also found their way into his paintings. Miró loved the company of poets—in fact, he often preferred it to the company of painters—and people who knew him in the 1920s have described how he sat as if hypnotized when his friends were talking their way toward a new kind of poetry in which reason would be suspended. In his art, as in their poems, conjunctions without precedent were made to seem the most natural thing in the world.

It was in 1954, when I was preparing material for *L'Œil*, that I got the

Constellation: Toward the Rainbow, 1941. Gouache and oil wash on paper, 18 x 15" (45.8 x 38 cm). Jacques and Natasha Gelman Collection.

Pasáje del Credito, Barcelona. Photo:
Gomis-Prats.

OPPOSITE:
Bench designed by Gaudí for Parc
Güell, Barcelona. Photo: Catalá-Roca.

idea of asking Miró, who often came to Paris for his graphic work, what I should show of his native city in my magazine. Somewhat to my surprise, he offered to show me around himself, so I set off from Paris with Brassaï, the photographer, and joined Miró and his wife, Pilar, in Barcelona.

Barcelona is the capital of Catalonia, a region very distinct from the rest of Spain, with its own history, its own heroes, its own language, its own literature, its own dance—the *sardana*—handed down from the Greeks. I soon found out that Catalans are passionately patriotic about their region and its accomplishments. Their own culture became even more precious to them in times of repression. Under Franco, even the Catalan language was banned. It is impossible to understand Miró without taking into account his almost religious veneration of his Catalan background.

We were to meet in Barcelona, where he still worked in an old building in Pasáje del Credito, just off the Ramblas in the Gothic section, where he was born. I had the address but didn't know the apartment number.

Miró was already a celebrated artist in France and America, and I presumed he was well known in his own country. However, there was no one in the little conical porter's lodge, so I went from floor to floor, knocking on doors and asking for "*el pintor Miró.*" No one had heard of him.

When I finally found him, what Miró wanted to show me first of all was the work of the visionary architect Antoní Gaudí. Gaudí was a passion of his—the embodiment of Catalan genius in all its singularity and invention. Miró took me first not to the well-known Sagrada Familia cathedral but to the park where he had played as a boy. (It was commissioned by Gaudí's major patron, Count Güell.) What Miró liked best about this park on the outskirts of the city was its total fantasy combined with precise calculation, technical ingeniousness combined with moments of pure improvisation. This could be a description of Miró's own way of working.

The park in question incorporates leaning columns of rough-textured stone and has a long terrace bordered by a serpentine bench in colors that sing out in the Catalan sunshine. When Gaudí worked there, funds were running low for materials (this often happened to him): a curved surface is expensive to cover. So Gaudí bought up odd lots of broken ceramics—fragments, bits of teapots, plates, bathroom tiles, anything—

RIGHT:
Detail of the bench designed by Gaudí,
Parc Güell. Photo: Catalá-Roca.

OPPOSITE:
Miró and the author in the Parc Güell,
1954. Photo: Brassaï.

Chimneys designed by Gaudí, Casa
Milá, Barcelona. Photo: Catalá-Roca.

and let his workmen invent mosaic patterns as they went along, setting
the pieces into the wet concrete of the bench: aleatory art *avant la lettre*.

As I looked closely with Miró at the details, I would notice little faces,
or motifs such as circles, which seemed to come right out of one of his
own compositions. In fact, as I went around with him, I began to see
through his eyes—everything turned into a Miró—even the round stop-
per of my bathtub with its two eyelike screws and lever for a nose
became a typical Miró personage.

After leaving the park, we went to visit a famous apartment building
designed by Gaudí around 1910, the Casa Milá. It has an arresting
façade, with undulating, chesty outlines, but Miró was even more
delighted with the imposing figures, like medieval knights, that function
as chimneys and ventilators on the top of the building.

We climbed up to the roof to see them. What touched Miró particularly was the fact that those astonishing sculptural forms cannot even be
seen from the street. Gaudí put them up there for his own sole pleasure
and amusement.

Then we trod what for Miró was hallowed ground—the museum of
Catalan art, above the town on Montjuïc. In that museum, Catalan
Romanesque frescoes, mostly from the twelfth century, had been
brought together from small churches—many of them derelict—in the
mountains.

LEFT:
Angel of the Apocalypse, twelfth century. Fresco. Museu d'Art de Catalunya, Barcelona.

RIGHT:
Last Judgment, twelfth century. Fresco. Museu d'Art de Catalunya, Barcelona.

OPPOSITE:
Figures and Constellations in Love with a Woman, 1941. Watercolor and gouache on paper, 18 x 15" (45.6 x 38 cm). Art Institute of Chicago, Gift of Gilbert W. Chapman, 1953.

This was the art that meant the most to Miró, and again and again it called forth a clicking of the tongue and an upward shake of the head in ecstatic approval. "I've been coming here since I was eight or ten years old," he said. "Every Sunday morning I used to come here by myself. These paintings were essential to me."

Many years later he asked me, "Do you recall the angels with eyes all over the place that we saw at the Museum of Catalan Art?" He made a vigorous gesture to indicate someone covered with eyes from head to foot. "Those were the Angels of the Apocalypse. I never forgot them."

Throughout Miró's work, eyes never cease to appear in unexpected places—in the middle of the sky, it might be, or sprouting on trees (page 233).

Another of his favorites in the Museum of Catalan Art was a Last Judgment with an angel weighing the hopeful against a scarlet background ablaze with gold stars. He pointed at the stars. "My childhood bedroom had stars painted on the ceiling. Stars have been with me all my life." And they did, indeed, become as integral to Miró's work as his own signature.

During that week in Barcelona, I learned as much about Miró as I did about his city. Often it was the most unlikely sight that sparked his inter-

Lintel in San Pablo del Campo,
Barcelona. Photo: Catalá-Roca.

BELOW:
Woman, Bird, 1977. Graphite on paper,
8¼ x 5⅞" (21 x 14.8 cm). Present
location unknown.

RIGHT:
Miró with graffiti, Barcelona, 1954.
Photo: Brassaï.

est and the tiniest detail that caught his eye. He was no chatterbox, and it was with just one word—"Look!"—that he responded to the little Romanesque church of San Pablo del Campo. He didn't mean the architecture, either; he meant the stone stars, set in circles, that had been carved on the lintel.

We visited the Sala del Tinell, the great Gothic hall where Ferdinand and Isabella received Columbus in 1493 on his return from the New World. It was impressive in its massive simplicity. But equally important to Miró was the line of flight of a bird overhead that stopped him in his tracks and filled him with wonder. And on one of our walks he stopped suddenly and looked fixedly at the spirals of a broken telephone wire that lay curled up on the hot asphalt of the road.

We went to the noble ruined vaults of the ancient shipyard where the boats were built that conquered the Turks at the Battle of Lepanto. But what he really liked was the display of pulleys in the Maritime Museum. Seen without him, those pulleys might have been just a group of pulleys; seen with him, they became perky, jaunty elements in a composition by Miró. But then, in his company, everything turned into a Miró.

Everything about the exuberance and the fantasy of Barcelona

LEFT:
Miró in a bar, Barcelona, 1954. Photo:
Brassaï.

RIGHT:
In the Kronenhalle restaurant, Zurich,
1955: *The Table (Still Life with Rabbit)*,
1920. Oil on canvas, 51⅛ x 43¼"
(130 x 110 cm).

delighted him, from the sallies of the local graffitists to the uninhibited spirals of Art Nouveau ironwork. He was particularly fond of the out-sized dragon that swung in the air above our heads, holding an umbrella in its claw, as a shop sign. Even our mid-morning glass of sherry was an adventure. Who else but Miró would have found a bar decorated with big stuffed animals hung with garlands of dried peppers?

Taking fire from Miró's example, I remembered his monumental still life of good things to eat that hangs in the Kronenhalle, a famous old Zurich restaurant. Gustav Zumsteg, who owns the Kronenhalle, ranks high among Swiss collectors, and he has always shared his collection with his customers. I had someone take a photograph of this painting, complete with two substantial citizens of Zurich eating their way through a memorable meal. Miró was delighted when I ran this photograph in *L'Œil*.

After those happy days in Barcelona, we ran a feature in *L'Œil* called "Miró Shows You Barcelona." He thoroughly enjoyed the idea. While I was putting Brassaï's photographs together with my text, I received a

Gouache with Motifs, 1954. Gouache on
paper, 19 x 26½" (48.3 x 67.3 cm).
Collection Rosamond Bernier, New
York.

large gouache from Miró. A score or more of emerald-green motifs, mingled with black ones, sparkled against the white paper. With the gouache came a note saying that he thought I might like to have some decorative elements for the pages of our joint feature.

"Just cut out the ones you like and paste them in the margins," he wrote. I cannot imagine any other artist, let alone one who is already world-famous, having the modesty to suggest that I should take his work apart in order to improve a layout. Naturally I did nothing of the sort, and have lived happily with the gouache ever since.

Thereafter, I was lucky enough to enjoy Miró's company all over the place—in Spain, in France, and in the United States. There are exactly twenty-five years between the photograph of the two of us at the beginning of this chapter and the one at the end of it.

Miró was reticent by nature, and his silences were legendary. But gradually he began to talk easily with the old friend that I had become. He was pleased with the conversations and interviews we had from time to time, and invariably at the end of each one of them he would say, "*Nous avons bien travaillé!*" We always spoke in French (although I can speak Spanish), because he was such a convinced and passionate Catalan that he refused to speak the Spanish of Castile, and I never got around to learning Catalan.

What follows here is something of what he told me about his life and times.

Miró's family owned a farm near Tarragona at Montroig, which means "Red Mountain." Its red earth had fed his imagination ever since he was a small boy. It was a magic place for him, and he went back periodically whenever he was depressed or exhausted or simply needed recharging.

"Elsewhere, everything is measured against Montroig. The fantastic mountains there play a big role in my life. It's not in the German Romantic sense. It is the shock of those forms on my spirit more than on my vision."

He was very isolated as a child. "There was a total separation between me and my parents. I felt this in a very painful, violent way. But I'm also very happy about it, because those difficulties gave me muscles. Hard times were ahead for me, and I needed those muscles."

The biographies always refer to a background of skilled artisans. A grandfather was a blacksmith, but Miró rather abruptly dismissed the

Vines and Olive Trees, Tarragona, 1919.
Oil on canvas, 28½ x 35⅝" (72.5 x
90.5 cm). Jacques and Natasha Gelman
Collection.

OPPOSITE:
Montroig, the Village and Church, 1919.
Oil on canvas, 28¾ x 24" (73 x 61 cm).
Private collection.

notion of his father's having been a fine goldsmith—"He repaired watches," he said dryly. His father didn't want to hear of his son's becoming an artist and insisted on apprenticing young Miró as a clerk in a business office. It is hard to imagine anything more unlikely. A complete nervous breakdown was the result, and Miró came back to Montroig to regain his stability.

His first paintings after art school were of his beloved Montroig. An old photograph shows houses huddled around the Romanesque church, with almond and olive trees in the foreground. The young artist kept closely to the motif, but in *Montroig, the Village and Church*, of 1919, we see how his particular vision heightened reality by baking the whole scene in uniformly brilliant Catalan light, tidying the fields with patchwork precision and stacking the buildings together with almost Cubist rigor. In an early landscape such as *Vines and Olive Trees, Tarragona*, also of 1919, he organized nature in terms of crisp and orderly detail.

Men, as men, play no part in Miró's titles. At most, they turn up under

Nude with Mirror, 1918. Oil on canvas, 44⅛ x 40⅛" (112 x 102 cm). Kunst-sammlung Nordrhein-Westfalen, Düsseldorf.

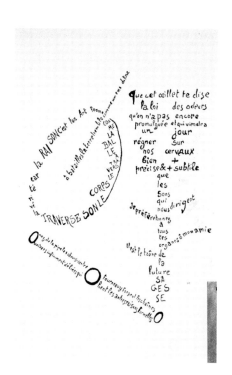

Guillaume Apollinaire, "La Guitare."

the ambiguous name of "personage." But women are there, over and over again. In his paintings, most often they are reinvented, and in ways that can be disconcerting, if not actually terrifying. But in that same period, he painted a straightforward nude with echoes of Cubism in her upper arms and torso, and of Matisse in the pink wall and the sharp pattern of stripes and fringe. The embroidered footstool on which she sits was still at Montroig when I went there.

I asked Miró what he knew of contemporary art before he went to Paris for the first time in 1919. At the Circulo de Sant Lluch, where he took art classes (Gaudí had gone there before him), there were two-hour sessions working from the model, Miró told me, with a fifteen-minute rest period in between. During the break the students would go to a nearby bookstore and look at albums with reproductions of Cézanne and van Gogh. Miró said that then he was swept away by van Gogh, but as time went by he was more and more lost in admiration before Cézanne.

He had seen what was then avant-garde work for the first time when his future dealer, Dalmau, showed the Cubists and the Douanier Rousseau, who appealed to Miró very much. Then, during World War I, the French Ministry for Cultural Affairs, through the dealer Ambroise Vollard, sent an exhibition of French Impressionists to Barcelona. (The Catalans have always been pro-French.) "I was dazzled," Miró told me. "It was overwhelming . . . almost a religious experience. I even was so overcome by a landscape by Monet that I took advantage of a moment when a guard wasn't there, and I went over and kissed it."

Things were stirred up generally when that truculent character Francis Picabia arrived in Barcelona from New York in 1917 and continued publishing his avant-garde magazine *391*. This gave Miró his first glimpse into the Dada world. It introduced him to the new French poetry as exemplified by Apollinaire's *calligrammes*—poems that made pictures with words.

Miró told me that when he went to Paris for the first time, he brought his self-portrait with him. He went to a little hotel (Hôtel de Rouen, in the rue Notre-Dame-des-Champs) where Catalan intellectuals stayed. It was kept by a charming old lady and her daughter, who was married to a Catalan. "Those people were magnificent. They rented me a room for a purely symbolic price, and they often invited me to lunch or dinner— I had very little money, so this was important."

He had planned to go to the Grande Chaumière, an open academy where one could draw from the model. But, he told me, "I received such an enormous shock at being in Paris, I was so overwhelmed that I was completely incapable of drawing a line. My hand was as if paralyzed—it was an intellectual paralysis. I was totally unable to work for some time."

So he gave up, and in the morning he went to the Louvre and in the afternoon he toured the galleries. "I hardly spoke French then, but every language was spoken in Montmartre. It was full of foreigners—Russians—and Foujita was there. Foujita was the big success then—busloads of Americans used to come and look at him!"

I asked Miró if it was then that he got to know Picasso. "Oh yes, I saw Picasso right away—the day after I arrived. I hadn't met him before, but I knew his mother very well: she was *formidable*, very much like him. She and my mother were friends."

"You never met in Barcelona?" I asked.

"He was twelve years older than I, and already famous; I didn't dare approach him. He came to Barcelona with Diaghilev and the Russian ballet company when they did *Parade*. He was in love with Olga Koklova, and they stayed at a hotel together, but he came home in the morning to visit his mother and to shave. I used to go see his mother, and one time she took me by the hand and said, 'Come with me,' and showed me the bathroom where he shaved. He had made a drawing on the mirror with his shaving brush and soap, and it stayed there—she had kept it piously.

"When I was leaving for Paris I went to see Picasso's mother and asked if she wanted me to take anything for her. 'Yes, yes,' she said, and she gave me a big Spanish cake for him. Next day, in Paris, I went and called and said, 'Monsieur Picasso, I bring this from your mother.'

"He wanted to see what I did, and from the first moment he was interested in me. He spoke to everyone—the dealers Daniel-Henry Kahnweiler and Paul Rosenberg—about me; he was very generous that way. But it didn't work, with the dealers. . . . Rosenberg was furious because I was staying in a shabby little room on the rue Delambre and he had to climb five flights to see me and the place was full of cockroaches."

I knew that Picasso owned two early Mirós—the self-portrait of 1919 and the 1921 *Portrait of a Spanish Dancer*—which are now in the Musée Picasso in Paris. The biographies say that Picasso bought these paintings to help out his young compatriot. It turned out that Picasso had never had to pay a penny for them. Miró's Barcelona dealer gave Picasso one picture, hoping to do business with him, and the other ended up with another dealer who owed money to Picasso and gave it to him in partial payment.

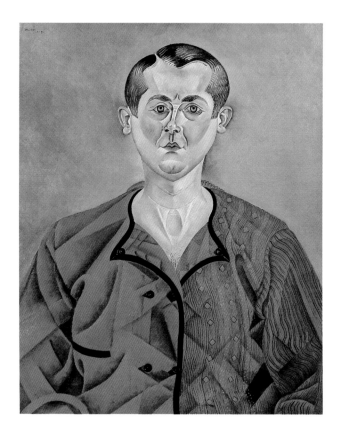

LEFT:
Portrait of a Spanish Dancer, 1921. Oil on canvas, 26 x 22" (66 x 56 cm). Musée Picasso, Paris.

RIGHT:
Self-Portrait, 1919. Oil on canvas, 28 ¾ x 23 ⅝" (73 x 60 cm). Musée Picasso, Paris.

I asked Miró whether he spoke Catalan, rather than Spanish, with Picasso, who was born in Spanish-speaking Málaga but grew up in Barcelona. Miró said that indeed they did speak Catalan together, and that Picasso's Catalan was fluent but that he spoke it with an accent. "What kind of accent?" I asked. "*Un accent de gendarme*," Miró said with a laugh. I never quite fathomed what that could be like.

By 1921, Miró was working on an enormous painting of the Montroig farm that was a loving inventory of farm life in microscopic detail: the buildings with their cracked walls, the farm animals, the barking dog, a woman washing clothes under a brilliant blue sky and steady sunshine. It may at first appear naive, but the composition is so skillful that the elements play off each other without confusion.

"When you painted *The Farm* and the earlier Montroig landscapes, did you work directly from nature?" I asked.

Miró smiled. "Oh yes, I used to work out of doors, like Cézanne! But take *The Farm:* everything I painted was really there, but I took liberties—I left off the wall of the chicken coop so that one could look inside— and there are lapses in scale. *The Farm* carried minute realism as far as I could take it."

Miró told me that he started this canvas in Montroig, continued it in

The Farm, Montroig, 1921–22. Oil on
canvas, 52 x 57⅞" (132 x 147 cm).
National Gallery of Art, Washington,
D.C.; Gift of Mary Hemingway.

Barcelona, and then took it to Paris, where he finished it. He also took an envelope to Paris with grasses from Montroig inside to copy; when the grasses dried up he had to go to the Bois de Boulogne and pick some more. He took nine months to give birth to that picture, he said, "working like a laborer, eight hours a day."

"How was the picture received in Paris?" I asked.

"Nobody liked it," Miró answered. "It was a very big picture, very hard to sell. I had no money, but I had to take a taxi to carry it to dealers—Paul Guillaume, Paul Rosenberg—and another taxi to bring it back. Rosenberg said, 'It's far too big—people live in small apartments. Why don't you cut it into several pieces?' "

"Then Ernest Hemingway bought it?"

"He bought it . . . for pennies, but he liked it a lot. He used to live in the rue Notre-Dame-des-Champs, near me, and I saw him often."

The Farmer's Wife, 1922–23. Oil on canvas, 31⅞ x 25⅝" (81 x 65 cm). Collection Madame Marcel Duchamp.

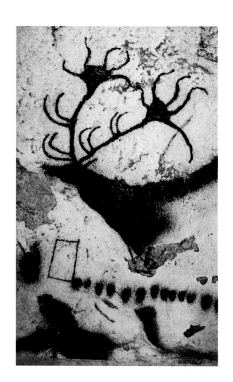

Petroglyph at Lascaux.

Miró said that he used to take very good care of himself physically to be in shape for his work—swimming summer and winter, walking and doing exercises—and that when he was in Paris he used to go to the Centre Américain to take boxing lessons, where Hemingway worked out, too. "It happened sometimes that we were in the ring together. He was huge, and I am very small—it made people smile."

In *The Farmer's Wife* (page 231), which dates from 1922–23, Miró kept to the kind of realism that can be so convincing in dreams: everything is uncannily clear but one element is monstrously out of scale. He had a mystical feeling about the earth as a source of life and strength, and here the farmer's wife shows her identification with the soil through her enlarged feet. "We Catalans think we must have our feet anchored firmly in the earth to be able to leap into the air to the stars," he said. This painting later belonged to Marcel Duchamp and still hangs in his widow's country house near Fontainebleau.

Miró painted *The Tilled Field, Montroig* in 1923–24. Although he was still drawing on the rich material of his family farm, imagination had overtaken—even transformed—reality, and most of the immediately recognizable elements had been codified into his personal shorthand. Miró had moved to Paris for part of every year and was in close contact with the Surrealists, both artists and writers. He admired the use of poetic metaphors by his writer friends, and he transferred what they did into a series of visual ideograms.

In *The Tilled Field*, a tree sprouts an eye and an enormous ear, a lizard pops up in a dunce cap. Miró's dual allegiance to Catalonia and Paris is celebrated by the Catalan flag and the tricolor on the left. The ox on the right reminds us of Miró's love for the prehistoric cave paintings of Lascaux and Altamira. This landscape has nothing to do with outside reality anymore, Miró said, but it is more Montroig than if he had done it from nature.

Miró had a little studio on the rue Blomet. He described it: he was always meticulous, and to the surprise of his more casual neighbors, the first thing he did was to whitewash his walls and go to the flea market for a few essentials, including a broom. And he put up some of the Catalan folk-art objects—figurines and straw toys—that he always liked to keep near him.

The painter André Masson, who had the studio next door, was a great reader. He introduced Miró to the world of French writing that was to be of the greatest importance to him. It was through Masson that Alfred Jarry's outrageous personage of Ubu, from his play *Ubu Roi*, became so

The Tilled Field, Montroig, 1923–24.
Oil on canvas, 26 x 36½" (66 x 92.7
cm). Solomon R. Guggenheim
Museum, New York.

much a part of Miró's being; many years later, Miró resurrected him in spirit when he designed costumes for a troupe of young Catalan actor-mimes called the Claca (page 268).

Through Masson, too, Stéphane Mallarmé became one of Miró's favorite poets; he was attentive not only to the music of the poet's words, but to the way they were sometimes dispersed across a page like random snowflakes. Miró also got to know the work of Rimbaud and Lautréamont, and among living writers he came to know Michel Leiris, Georges Limbour, Robert Desnos, and Antonin Artaud. Miró told me emphatically that this immersion in the world of French writing meant infinitely more to him than his contact with painters.

Masson was a helpful friend and, like Picasso, tried to interest dealers in the young Catalan. One of his friends was Jacques Doucet, now known as a couturier, as the founder of a major art library in Paris, and as a collector who was the first owner of Picasso's *Les Demoiselles d'Avignon*. At Masson's instigation, Doucet went to look at Miró's work. "*Mais il est fou, votre voisin,*" was Doucet's reaction: "But your neighbor's crazy."

With Masson, Miró used to go to a little Bal Nègre nearby. Miró didn't dance, but he enjoyed watching. Juan Gris used to come every night, Miró told me: "He was an indefatigable dancer. I wondered when he had time to paint."

André Breton and his Surrealists were impressed with the total originality of Miró's vision—here was someone who had a hot line to the marvelous. His first Paris exhibition was sponsored by the whole group.

Contact with the Surrealists in the middle twenties was a very intense experience for him, Miró said, but he remained somewhat apart from the group's activities. He never plunged into their feuds and their noisier manifestations. But their emphasis on poetry, on the unconscious, on the accidental, on chance was of fundamental importance for him. Pure automatism, however, never interested Miró—only chance controlled.

"What about André Breton?" I asked him. "I was never close to Breton," Miró said. "His dogmatic side exasperated me. He wanted what he saw to prove what he had written."

"Which of the Surrealists were you closest to?" I asked. "Paul Eluard, a very great poet," he answered unhesitatingly. "Eluard's poetry captivated me, and with him one lived in an atmosphere of pure poetry." Eluard, for his part, had been writing about Miró since 1926. And Miró undertook to illustrate Eluard's *A Toute Epreuve* with real fervor. It resulted in a superb, festive interplay between word and image.

It was the contact with poetry that led Miró to introduce words into his painting, he told me. "I still do it. . . . I already loved the poetry of Apollinaire when I was twenty, and he used words as poem-pictures in his *calligrammes*. I had been very struck by one, 'L'Horloge de Demain,' in *391*—Picabia's magazine—printed in several colors with different-size type for the words. I was captivated by his *Le Poète Assassiné*—I used to read it during my military service between shifts of guard duty."

In the mid-twenties Miró began to simplify his images. Where there had been two hundred clues to what he was up to, there were suddenly only a few. In 1925 he made several paintings called *Head of a Catalan Peasant*. An early one is still full of clues; in a later one they have evaporated. He gave his paintings a blue background, like a Catalan sky

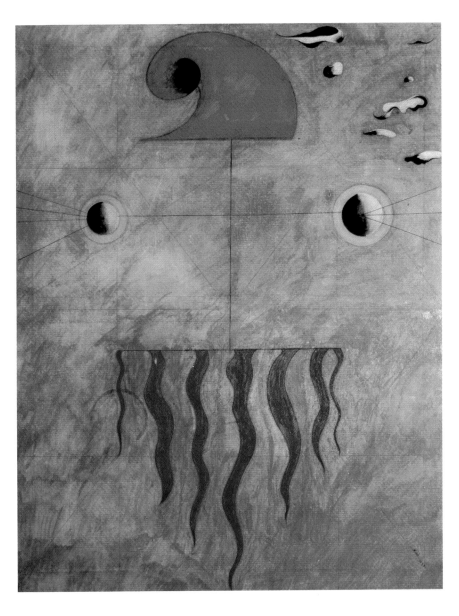

Painting, 1925. Oil on canvas, 34¼ x 45¼" (77 x 113.9 cm). Collection Rosamond Bernier, New York.

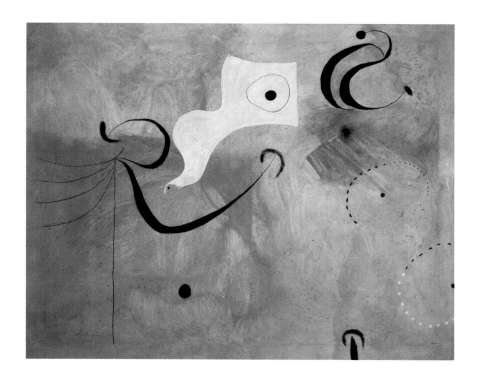

stretched taut, and he just touched in the essentials: the two eyes that missed nothing, the cap, the beard, the pipe.

His paintings got less and less busy, until in the end there was nothing there except a pure blue background, brushed ever more thinly, and one or two calligraphic incidents that floated, seemingly weightless, in a dimensionless yonder. Often they seem to have been as much threaded as painted, with a hair-thin line and a brief pecking motion of the brush.

Miró at this time saw a photograph that struck him. Instead of reproducing it or making a collage out of it, he simply wrote the word "Photo" in careful sign-painter script on his canvas in its place. And beneath a small cloud of his favorite blue he wrote: "This is the color of my dreams." He cared particularly about this picture. It used to belong to Max Ernst.

In the 1960s Miró made several visits to New York. On one occasion Robert Rauschenberg, by nature the most expansive and hospitable of men, gave him a party. Miró spoke no English but enjoyed the occasion. He was particularly touched when Rauschenberg suddenly picked up a pot of blue paint and slung it at the glass skylight, turning it blue by way of tribute to Miró's *This Is the Color of My Dreams*. "This is for you," he said to Miró. "He did that," Miró told me. "I was deeply moved."

After the rue Blomet studio, Miró moved to the rue Tourlaque, where he put up a sign on his door, TRAIN PASSANT SANS ARRÊT—"The train doesn't stop here"—and where he had Jean Arp, Max Ernst, René

This Is the Color of My Dreams, 1925.
Oil on canvas, 38 x 51" (96.5 x 129.5
cm). Private collection.

Magritte, and Paul Eluard as neighbors. Arp was the artist who resembled Miró most closely, and the two had many affinities. "We shared each other's poverty and radishes," Miró said. Certainly Miró's fluid shapes were similar in feeling to Arp's drifting clouds and swelling plant forms. A 1924 wood relief by Arp makes the point.

Miró's face would light up when he talked of his old friend Alexander Calder. They got to know each other well in the twenties and thirties, when Calder was living in Paris. "We were very, very close for over forty years. Someone with such humanity." Calder's celebrated circus with its miniature movable wire figures was a great bond between them.

"He came to Montroig with his little circus," Miró remembered, "and he gave a performance for the farmers. Unforgettable! This huge man with the tiny figures, and his incredible manual dexterity! It was very hot, and he pulled out a pair of scissors and—crac, crac, crac—he cut off the arms and legs of his clothes!"

Miró made a number of circus pictures in 1927, probably inspired by his friend. He never liked complicated interpretations of his images. When a very determined young curator tried to probe into the sexual connotations of the white shape in one of them, he said, "Oh no, it's just a horse."

Between the two friends, ideas flew back and forth. Calder owned several paintings by Miró; one of them was *Three Women* of 1935. Miró and

Painting, 1927. Oil on canvas, 38⅛ x 51⅛" (97 x 130 cm). Tate Gallery, London.

Calder had in common, among much else, both a sharp eye for the everyday elements of our visual experience and a gift for their metamorphosis. Miró's forms lead a vivid life of their own on the canvas, but we can also imagine them bouncing off an imaginary trampoline and landing in the topmost branches of a Calder mobile.

Because of financial difficulties, Miró spent the spring of 1933 back in Barcelona, in his parents' house. There he worked in a little attic room arranged as a studio. He had become fascinated with illustrations of machine tools in catalogues and newspapers, and in his usual meticulous way, cut them out and pasted them carefully on large sheets of white paper. He strung these up in his workroom—there were to be eighteen in all. As he looked at them, they stopped being banal objects and slipped into a new identity: elements in a Miró composition.

Miró made one of those luminous atmospheric backgrounds of his, and transcribed the machine forms into his own configurations. Sometimes they suggest beasts from the prehistoric cave paintings he so admired.

It would be a mistake to consider Miró's work all gentle humor and whimsy. He was eaten alive by his visions—a man who saw deep into human nature and was often appalled by what he saw. Terror and ferocity, anguish and foreboding are never absent from his work for long, and

OPPOSITE, TOP:
Collage (study for *Painting*, 1933), 1933. Cut-and-pasted photomechanical reproductions with pencil, 18½ x 24⅞" (47 x 63.2 cm). Collection, The Museum of Modern Art, New York; Gift of the artist.

OPPOSITE, BOTTOM:
Painting, 1933. Oil on canvas, 51⅜ x 64" (130.5 x 162.5 cm). Fundació Joan Miró, Barcelona.

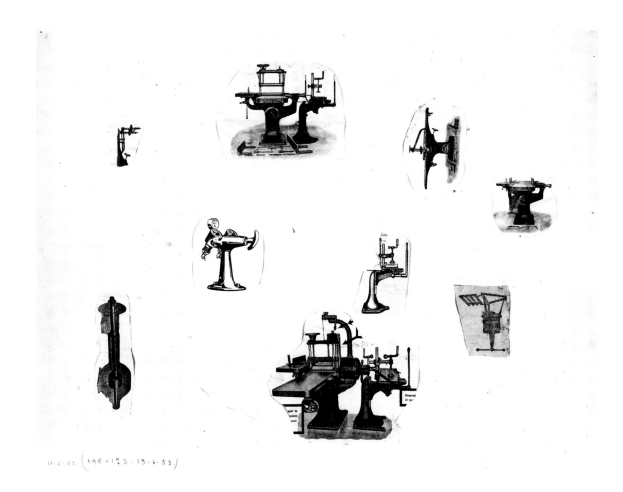

11·2·33. (195×173 · 13·6·33.)

Rope and People I, 1935. Oil on cardboard mounted on wood, with coil of rope, 41¼ x 29⅜" (105 x 74.6 cm. Collection, The Museum of Modern Art, New York; Gift of the Pierre Matisse Gallery.

the plight of the individual in the twentieth century has found few chroniclers as resourceful as he.

In the mid-1930s, as though anticipating the horrors of the Spanish Civil War, he made a rope collage surrounded by fierce figures. Miró saw the rope as an instrument of torture. The figures are also torturing themselves: the man on the left is biting his own hand.

When Man Ray photographed Miró for the Surrealist publication *Minotaure*, he had the insight to incorporate in the image what looks like a hangman's rope. Although Miró appeared the most tranquil and angelic of men, he was subject to corrosive depressions and violence of feeling. This aspect of his personality was kept well hidden in his studio.

The outbreak of the Spanish Civil War affected Miró profoundly. He

Miró with Rope, mid-1930s. Photo: Man Ray.

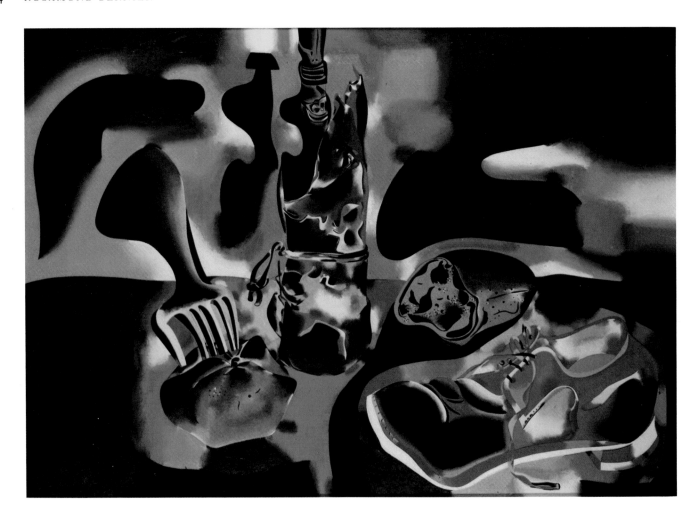

Still Life with Old Shoe, 1937. Oil on canvas, 32 x 46" (81.3 x 116.4 cm). Collection, The Museum of Modern Art, New York; James Thrall Soby Bequest.

did not play an active political role, but he expressed his despair in two direct statements. *Still Life with Old Shoe*, from 1937, is a return to realism, long left behind, but a tragic realism quite unlike that of his early Catalan landscapes. As if clinging to real objects were the only path to sanity, during this crisis in his feelings Miró had gone back to drawing from the model, like a student, at the Grande Chaumière.

Then he set up a still-life arrangement in the gallery of his dealer, Pierre Loeb (he was in between studios). Every day he came to paint, and he went on working at it for months. He took simple elements to speak for the sufferings of the common people, emblems of endurance: an apple pierced by an outsized fork, a bottle of wine that looks as if it had been wrapped in blackened bandages, a half-eaten loaf of bread, patently stale, an old beat-up shoe (van Gogh's painting of boots was a favorite of his). This was his *Guernica*, but where Picasso had used black and white for his picture of indignation painted the same year, Miró suffused his still life with sinister, lurid color. The broadsheet called *Aidez*

Aidez l'Espagne, 1937. Broadsheet, 12¼ x 9¼" (31.1 x 23.5 cm). Collection Rosamond Bernier, New York.

l'Espagne, showing a Catalan peasant with gigantic clenched fist, was sold to raise money for the Republicans.

During the first winter of World War II, Miró took his wife and small daughter to a house he rented near the sea in Normandy, not far from his friend Georges Braque. In Miró's luggage was an album of particularly beautiful sheets of paper. Like everyone else in the area, he was subject to very stringent blackout regulations. "I had always enjoyed looking out of the window at night and seeing the sky and the stars and the moon, but now we weren't allowed to do that anymore, so I painted the windows blue, and I took up my brushes and paints, and that was the beginning of the *Constellations*."

When he had finished work for the day on his oil paintings, Miró dipped his brushes in gasoline and wiped them on those same sheets of particularly beautiful paper. Something in his imagination was fired by the accidental marks that resulted, and gradually, while the world outside generated an atmosphere of ever greater foreboding, he began what might well have been a last roundup of all the ideas and all the images that were dearest to him. He called these paintings the *Constellations*. First he drew them fast and freely in charcoal. Then he began to paint them in gouache, with a watchmaker's care and precision.

They were small sheets—eighteen by fifteen inches—but he took a month or more on every one of them (pages 212, 219, and opposite). The images were multitudinous, as if each painting were a refugee ship that had to be filled to the last square inch of standing room. Nothing was left out: birds, beasts, insects, stars, emblematic men and women, the sky, the sun, and the moon.

In the spring of 1940, Miró and his family got away from the advancing German armies—none too soon—and managed to catch the last train out of Paris to Barcelona. Even in Barcelona, Miró was not safe from those who sided with the Germans, and the family went on to Majorca, where the *Constellations* were eventually completed.

The *Constellations* had long, poetic titles, but those titles were not chosen at random. For instance, a careful look at *The Beautiful Bird Deciphering the Unknown to a Pair of Lovers*, will reveal that all of the elements are right there: the bird with its parrot's beak flies in the upper right, its head pointing left. The big woman towers on the right, with a black-and-red vagina and whirligig eyes where her breasts should be. On the left is her pint-sized lover with a hair or two sprouting from his nose and forehead.

The *Constellations* were among the first works of art from Europe to reach New York at the end of the war. They came to the Pierre Matisse Gallery by diplomatic pouch. Pierre Matisse had championed Miró's work in this country for many years, most memorably in times when no one wanted it, and he always remembered that the all-over, deemphasized configurations of these little paintings had a great effect on the American artists who came to see them.

As of the end of World War II, it began to be understood in the United States that Miró was an artist of the first rank. There had been some enlightened interest as far back as 1931, when the Arts Club of Chicago gave Miró his first show in the United States. But the Depression had really taken hold by 1933, when the Pierre Matisse Gallery had a very

OPPOSITE:
Constellation: The Beautiful Bird Deciphering the Unknown to a Pair of Lovers, 1941. Gouache and oil wash on paper, 18 x 15" (45.8 x 38 cm). Collection, The Museum of Modern Art, New York; Acquired through the Lillie P. Bliss Bequest.

beautiful exhibition of paintings done by Miró. Only one work was sold, despite Matisse's unstinting efforts to interest museums and collectors. (It was an inspired museum director, Everett A. Austin, Jr., who bought that one for the Wadsworth Atheneum in Hartford, Connecticut.)

In 1947, Pierre Matisse arranged for Miró and his wife to make their first visit to the United States. The pretext was a commission for a mural in the restaurant of the Terrace Plaza Hotel in Cincinnati. "I didn't very much like the idea of my work hanging in a restaurant," Miró told me, "but Pierre always assured me that it would end up in the Cincinnati Art Museum, and it did."

While he was working on the mural, the Mirós lived in New York in a borrowed studio on 119th Street. "The Calders loved to dance," Miró remembered, "and I don't know how to dance at all. They took me to a big place in Harlem—the Savoy Ballroom, with wonderful music.

"It was all right to go to Harlem in those days, but as I could not speak a word of English, Sandy told me to be careful not to offend anyone by showing I didn't understand them. Sandy and his wife, Louisa, were dancing away, and I was alone at the table, when a magnificent black woman came up and asked me to dance. She was really superb, and twice as tall as I am. I didn't dare refuse. So . . ." Miró stood up and demonstrated by just how much she had towered above him.

Thanks to his fellow Catalan José-Luis Sert, Miró painted his first university mural in the United States in 1950, for the graduate center at Harvard. Thereafter, museums and collectors in New York and elsewhere in the United States were much more responsive to Miró's work than were their counterparts in Europe. In 1959 he had his second retrospective at the Museum of Modern Art, and President Eisenhower presented him with the Guggenheim International award at the White House. But Miró told me in 1980 that until recently there was exactly one work by him in any public collection in Paris, and that was one he had presented himself. Nor was it until 1978 that he had any official recognition in Spain.

To the end of his life, Miró regarded the United States with wonder and awe. Its very place names were magical to him. Once, when I called him long distance on New Year's Day, he asked where I was calling from. "Texas," I replied. "*Texas!*" he said, drawing the word out as if he didn't want to let go of it. If I had been calling from the moon, I could not have impressed him more.

In the mid-1950s, when I first knew him, Miró embarked on a new adventure: making ceramics with an old classmate from Barcelona art school days, Artigas, the master potter. Miró was always stimulated by working with skilled craftsmen, whether making engravings or tapestries, and he was exhilarated by the collective nature of the proceedings. He would hole up for months at a time in Gallifa, a mountain village outside Barcelona with no electricity, no telephone, where Artigas and his son—there was no one else—had a kiln in their eighteenth-century farmhouse. He started out making all kinds of pots, plaques, small sculptures, enjoying what he called "the battle against fire" and exploring the peculiarities of the medium, "not simply painting on another material."

Photographs show Miró working away like an attentive schoolboy. They also show some of the first small pieces that were fired, and the artist actually taking possession of the terrain by painting his signs directly on the stones of the courtyard.

Artigas told me that Miró was so excited by the craggy rocks of Gallifa that he went out and painted right on them for his own pleasure. "I was incorporating myself with the elements," Miró said. The great

Miró at the ceramic studio in Gallifa, mid-1950s. Photo: Sabine Weiss for *L'Œil.*

OPPOSITE:
Miró painting on flagstones, Gallifa, mid-1950s. Photo: Sabine Weiss for *L'Œil*.

The Wall of the Sun, 1957–58. Ceramic, 9' 10⅛" x 24' 7¼" (3 x 7.5 m). UNESCO headquarters, Paris.

weathered vinegar-red rocks reminded him of Montroig and inspired him to make rocklike shapes in ceramics.

These first small-scale experiments led to vast ceramic murals and eventually to large-scale sculpture. What interested Miró was art in a public context that would be seen by many people. He was able to achieve exactly that in the walls of ceramic tile that he made for the Paris headquarters of UNESCO in 1957.

In the mid-fifties Miró left Barcelona for Majorca. He had been "discovered" by the Spanish establishment when he won first prize at the Venice Biennale of 1954, and he didn't like the attention or the disturbances. For many years he had had to work in cramped quarters and had dreamed of a big studio. Now he had it, next to his house near Palma, built by his friend José-Luis Sert; outside were terraces planted with olive trees and a view over the water. When I went to see him there, he had just moved in, but he had already made the courtyard unmistakably his by adding a few old farm implements and a wheel.

Here at last was room for the big pictures he wanted to paint. But,

OPPOSITE, TOP:
Miró's atelier in Majorca, mid-1950s.
Photo: Roland Penrose.

OPPOSITE, BOTTOM:
Miró's atelier in Majorca, 1969. Photo:
Arnold Newman.

Miró told me, at first the very perfection of it threw him off completely. "I was frightened, when I saw the atelier finished. I was seized with panic. I felt vertigo in front of all that space."

Miró was almost fanatically neat. The painting materials were laid out in orderly fashion. Pots with brushes sticking out of them were lined up with military precision. Soon there were scores of canvases in all stages of progress. One canvas had a small pencil sketch pinned onto it—an idea for the future. Notes in black and red and clippings were filed under stones on a flat table like butterflies come to rest. Miró had just bought some cheap oils, views of Barcelona, at the flea market and was painting over them. He liked backgrounds that somehow jogged his imagination.

He was at last able to unpack his belongings that had been stored in Paris since before the war and take stock. "When I took out works dating back over years and years, I began to make my autocriticism," he told me. "I corrected myself coldly, objectively, the way a teacher at the Grande Chaumière corrects a pupil. I was pitiless with myself. I destroyed an enormous number of canvases, and especially drawings and gouaches. I would look at a whole series, then put them aside to be burned, then—zac, zac, zac—I tore them up. There were several big 'purges' like that over several years. Some of the old canvases I wanted to rework, others I wanted to leave as they were; I left them against the wall of my studio so I could look at them and not lose contact. The work I did after that resulted from what I learned during this period."

He told me that one of the old canvases he reworked was a self-portrait from 1937 to 1938 (page 254). When Miró had gone back to investigating the world of real objects in those years—drawing from the model again—he made his own portrait, exploring himself for the first time in almost twenty years. "I took one of those magnifying mirrors that are used for shaving; I drew everything I saw, very minutely. Then I made a very large drawing, bigger than life." What Miró didn't say is that however literal he thought his drawing to be, he managed to convey his visionary quality—sparks and flames seem to envelop the figure.

This picture was sold and went off to America. Miró was sad to lose it. So he took a photograph of the drawing to an architect friend, who made an enlargement on squared-off paper, to the dimensions of the original picture. The reproduction was in one of the cases Miró now unpacked. In 1960, he set about painting a new version on top of the reproduction—a change of focus, he called it. He added heavy black lines, ghoulish eyes, a head sprouting three hairs. Was his intention to mock the obsessional, lyrical character of the earlier work? He didn't say.

But he did say that he cared deeply about it and was keeping it for himself.

In spite of his initial misgivings, Miró said the studio soon became "*archicomble*, like a forest."

I asked him how he worked. Did he still start early in the morning?

"Ah, yes," he replied. "It's early in the morning that I see things clearly, that I'm most lucid. I actually start very early, very intensely, in bed. I go to bed about eleven o'clock, and I wake up at four and at that time think of what I did the day before and what I must do this day. I plan my work. Then I go back to sleep. But it's between four and five that things get going.

"I get up about eight, and after breakfast I go to my atelier and work until two. I have lunch, I rest for twenty minutes, then I go back to the studio—and stay all afternoon.

"The most tiring work is done in the morning. The afternoon, I look at what I've done, I pull out the weeds, I prepare the work for the next day. I store up ideas like seeds—some of them grow, others don't. And I do other things . . . if I have to make a cover, or an engraving. . . .

"I always have a great quantity of canvases in my atelier, maybe a hundred. Some I leave resting, partly worked, for years. Little by little they mature—and one day, I go into the studio without a preconceived idea. There will be a number of canvases against the wall, and I'm called by one of them, and I take it up again. It is *un appel magnétique*"—a magnetic force—"drawing me, or an electric discharge, if you want. I am forced, compelled. It is a physical thing.

"Then I attack"—Miró made the noise of someone charging. "Then intellectual work establishes the equilibrium. The equilibrium of forms, and colors, and volumes. One line calls for another, one color asks for another. After that I rest, and the next day, with a fresh mind, I judge what I have done."

Miró insisted that when he was working nobody—and that really meant *nobody*—could come into the studio. "I'm always alone there. No assistant. Never any music. Silence." For that reason I cannot confirm what he told me more than once: that when he got into the studio and closed the door he was really beside himself. "I go completely wild. The older I get, the meaner and the more aggressive I get." I must add that if this was so, outside the studio there was never a trace of it.

The Bird with a Calm Gaze, Its Wings in Flames, 1952. Oil on canvas, 31⅞ x 39⅜" (81 x 100 cm). Private collection.

"I like it that the public still reacts aggressively to my work. When someone went to my show at the Grand Palais in Paris and said that I should have my hands cut off, that encouraged me to go on working."

For someone who normally radiated benignity, dressed with an English elegance, and was uncomfortable unless he was perfectly shaven, Miró was indeed a man beside himself when he got into the studio. He always kept certain things around him—placed with the precision of his signs on a canvas, pinned up, or on shelves—that contained some sort of provocative message for him. Everything he touched became a Miró, as happened on one of his atelier walls with a starfish, a sea horse, some fishing hooks, and a stalk of wheat. The arrangement is not unlike his 1924 painting *Maternity*.

ABOVE:
A wall of Miró's studio. Photo: Gomis-Prats.

RIGHT:
Maternity, 1924. Oil on canvas, 35⅛ x 29⅛" (91 x 74 cm). Private collection, London.

Majorcan whistles owned by Miró.

Among his treasures were Catalan straw toys and folk figurines, such as the sprightly Majorcan painted whistles—directly descended from archaic Mediterranean sculpture—on which he enjoyed giving a vigorous toot. Much of his own art remained close to the spontaneous, anonymous tradition of folk art, as the painting on page 255 testifies. But it also has more distant affinities.

Miró often told me how deeply he cared about prehistoric cave art: the paintings of Lascaux and Altamira and the petroglyphs at Pech-Merle. He liked to use the imprint of his own hand dipped in paint on a canvas—the same motif that appears in cave art in many countries.

In 1960, as if suddenly reminded of his evanescent blue-field paintings of the mid-twenties, Miró gave up the seduction of his small signs (the *Constellations* and what followed them) to do a series of very large paintings, serene and weightless, of limitless space, using the simplest possible means (pages 258, 259). They marked a return to painting after his reappraisal of his own work when he took over the new studio in Palma. With a few black spots, a bar of red, or a line that hovers before our eyes like a kite string, Miró takes us into unexplored depths.

He talked to me at length about these works at that time. His purpose was not decorative. He wanted to suggest an infinity which in former paintings had been symbolized by what he called "the ladder of escape." The new paintings took a very long time, not to paint, but to meditate, he said. "It took an enormous effort, a great interior tension, to arrive at the desired spareness."

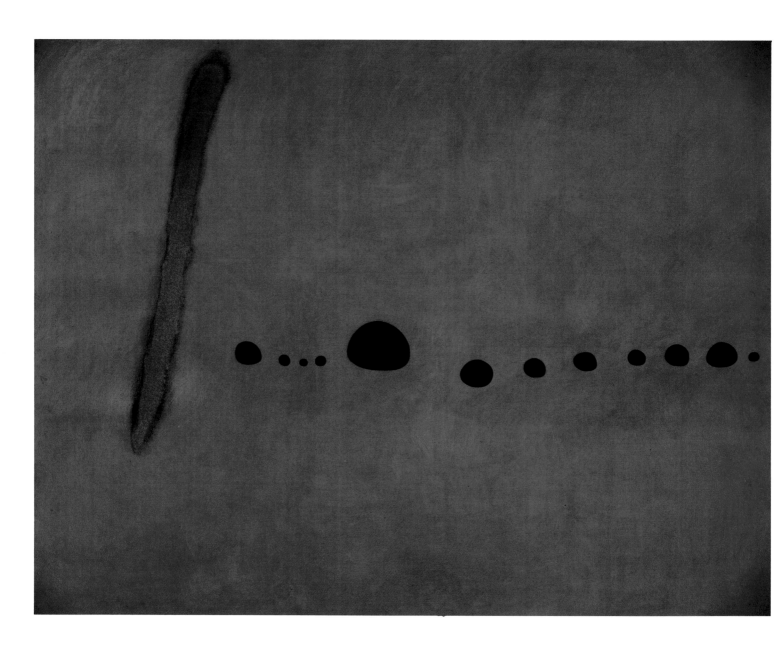

Blue II, 1961. Oil on canvas,
8' 10¼" x 11' 7¾" (2.7 x 3.55 m).
Musée National d'Art Moderne, Centre
Georges Pompidou, Paris.

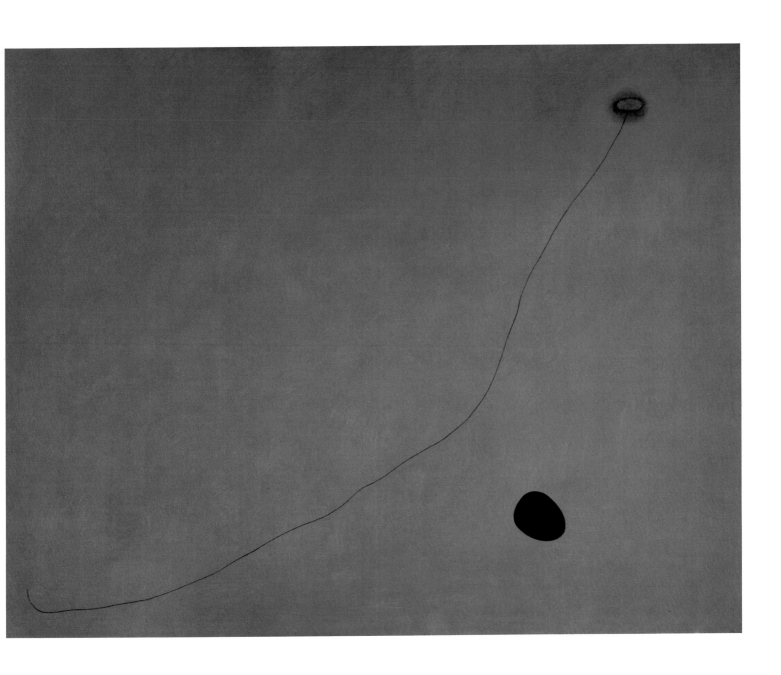

Blue III, 1961. Oil on canvas, 8' 10¼" x
11' 7¾" (2.7 x 3.55 m). Musée National
d'Art Moderne, Centre Georges Pompidou, Paris.

"The preliminary state was an intellectual one. It was like preparing for a religious rite. . . . You know how Japanese archers get ready for competition. They start by putting themselves into a particular state of mind: they exhale, inhale, exhale. It was the same for me. I knew that I risked everything: one weakness, one error, and everything would have fallen apart.

"I began by drawing in charcoal, very early in the morning. All the rest of the day I was preparing myself, and finally I started to paint. First the background. But it wasn't simply a question of placing the color, like a housepainter; all the movements of the brush, the wrist, the respiration of the hand intervened, too. The combat exhausted me."

In 1968 and 1969, Miró's native city got the chance to enjoy large exhibitions of his work for the first time (he was well over seventy). Enthusiasm in Barcelona was tremendous, and the younger generation could see that he was the youngest of them all. It meant a great deal to Miró that the 1969 exhibition was held in a noble old Gothic building, once the Santa Cruz hospital, now a library. It was here that, in 1926, Gaudí was brought to die, unrecognized, after being run over by a streetcar.

Among the vigorous paintings from this period is *Women and Birds in the Night*. Miró's night skies are often white, and the moon and even the sun become black or laden with color.

Miró's titles often include the word "bird." I asked him about this. "I was always fascinated by birds. The line of flight of small birds is very moving to me. For example, at Montroig, there is a plain—I see it well—a plain planted with grapevines—the earth, the horizon, the sky, the passage of a bird—zzzzzzz." He repeated to himself, like an invocation: "The earth, the horizon, the sky, the passage of a bird. . . . It has such beauty."

Another theme that dominates his work is night. "I'm overwhelmed when I see, in an immense sky, the crescent moon, stars. . . . I like nocturnal lights, factories at night, the world seen from a plane at night. I owe one of the greatest emotions of my life to a night flight over Washington. . . . Seen from a plane, a city is a marvelous thing."

I asked Miró about the fact that his titles were always in French. "My intellectual formation, the contact with poetry, came in Paris. I still think in French for intellectual work, while my intimate notes are in Catalan." "Never in Spanish?" "*Ah non*, I am a Catalan. Spanish, other parts of

Women and Birds in the Night, 1968.
Oil on canvas, 80¾ x 76¾" (205 x 195
cm). Private collection.

Spain, cities like Madrid—they are as foreign to me as . . . Holland."

Miró was not a collector. Unlike Picasso, he never bought anyone else's paintings. But he did make some exchanges. I remember two Légers and a Braque in his Palma living room, and he also had a Kandinsky that he was very happy with.

"I knew Kandinsky well when he came to live in Paris. He was a refugee at the time, and was very badly treated by idiots who knew nothing about him or his work. In the spiritual sense, he had a certain influence on me. His writings interested me from an aesthetic point of view, but it was to the man himself, and the vibrations that emanated from him, that I responded most."

He had the greatest admiration for Matisse. When I saw Miró not long after the "Paris-Moscow" exhibition at the Pompidou Center in Paris, he told me he had been bowled over by the Matisses. "I had never seen the Matisses that are in Russia. The *Dance*, especially—how fabulous it is! What a great artist! I wish I had seen him more often. But I was shy, and hesitated to disturb him."

He was deeply moved when I reminded him of what Matisse had said when Louis Aragon asked him whom he considered a true painter among contemporary artists: "Miró, yes, Miró . . . because it doesn't matter what he represents on his canvas, but if in a certain place he put a red spot, you can be sure that it had to be there and not anywhere else. Take it away and the painting collapses."

A personal moment from the early seventies is recorded on page 163. Once I went to see Miró after he had learned that through a personal upheaval I had lost my entire library. He looked stricken at my misfortune. Without a word of explanation he disappeared into his study and eventually reappeared carrying a copy of the major book on his work, by Jacques Dupin. He had made me an exuberant color drawing on the opening page. It may look as if it had been dashed off, but he had been gone a full half-hour.

Not long afterward he took me out for a seafood dinner at one of his favorite Barcelona restaurants, with so many previously unknown-to-me local monsters to eat that I suspected he had designed them himself. We were in a cheerful mood after drinking respectable quantities of Priorato, the deep red wine from his beloved Montroig—if you drink enough of it, you even understand Catalan. He was amused to order a local cheese for me that looked like a Claes Oldenburg sculpture of a woman's collapsed breast.

By Miró's eighty-fifth year, 1978, Franco was dead. For the first time

Title page of the 1978 Madrid exhibition catalogue, inscribed by Miró. Collection Rosamond Bernier, New York.

Opening page of *Joan Miró: Life and Work*, by Jacques Dupin, inscribed by Miró. Collection Rosamond Bernier, New York.

Spain was ready to give its most celebrated living artist an official apotheosis, and for the first time Miró felt that he could accept it. I was there for the excitement, and it was very satisfying to find two vast retrospective exhibitions drawing full houses in Madrid, even though the guest of honor—characteristically—left town as soon as the official openings were over.

One of the Madrid exhibitions was organized by the Fundació Joan Miró. Like Matisse, Picasso, and Léger, Miró now had a museum named after him, which everyone who loves his work will want to visit. It is in Barcelona, and Miró presented it with a great many of his works in all

Title page of the 1979 Maeght Founda-
tion exhibition catalogue, inscribed by
Miró. Collection Rosamond Bernier,
New York.

pour

Bernier)

Rosamond

avec la vieille et

sincère amitié de

Miró!

10 VII. 79.

**joan
miró**

PEINTURES   SCULPTURES
DESSINS   CÉRAMIQUES
1956 - 1979

7 juillet - 30 septembre 1979

fondation maeght
06570 saint-paul

OPPOSITE:
The Smile of a Tear, 1973. Oil on
canvas, 79 x 79" (200.7 x 200.7 cm).
Private collection.

media. But he didn't even like to give it its official name. "A museum-
monument is a dead thing," he used to say. "What I want is to be a pretext for those who come after me." He saw the Miró Foundation not as
his consecration but as a study center for living art, a place where young
people could go to exhibitions, hear music, see movies, and invent the
future. It was designed by his friend José-Luis Sert.

In 1979 a Miró exhibition was held at the Fondation Maeght in Saint-
Paul-de-Vence, in the south of France. It consisted of work from the previous twenty-two years. It was exhilarating to see that in old age he was
neither weakened nor depleted. Those late paintings (pages 265–267)
showed as clearly as ever the power, the eloquence, and the nobility that
he could bring to subject matter that had been reduced and reduced
again, like some masterpiece of the *nouvelle cuisine*.

To Miró's delight it had been arranged that a little company of young

OPPOSITE:
Catalan Peasant by Moonlight, 1968.
Acrylic on canvas, 63 ¾ x 51 ⅛" (162 x
130 cm). Fundació Joan Miró,
Barcelona.

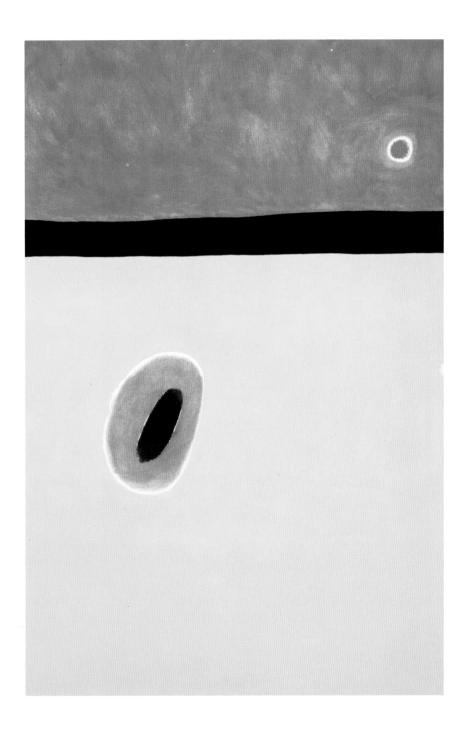

RIGHT:
*The Lark's Wing Encircled by Blue of
Gold Joins the Heart of the Poppy on the
Prairie of Diamonds*, 1967. Oil on can-
vas, 76 ¾ x 51 ⅛" (194.9 x 129.8 cm).
Private collection.

Catalan actor-mimes, the Claca, would perform in the Foundation gardens during the exhibition. He had been carried away by their verve and by their improvisations, which followed an old Catalan tradition of street theater—a cross between raucous Punch and Judy shows and the giant figures that are still paraded through towns and villages for the feast of Corpus Christi.

With characteristic generosity—particularly toward the young—he undertook to design costumes and props for them. He didn't just design their costumes on paper. He painted directly on the white cloth and foam-rubber props, cut to his specifications, which they were wearing. Sometimes he delicately added a star. Sometimes he sloshed whole bucketfuls of paint at them with ferocious, gleeful vigor. The costumes were like huge, animated Miró sculptures, encasing the actors in carapaces culminating in an outrageously enlarged nose or limb.

Naturally I went to Saint-Paul-de-Vence to see the exhibition and to

Miró at work on Claca costumes.

Claca costume designed by Miró.

spend some time with Miró. When I arrived at the Foundation, a French television crew was filming a rehearsal of the Claca. Contrasting with the bloated, multicolored costumes was the artist himself: small, impeccable in his white suit, face as shiny and rosy as a ripe nectarine, round blue eyes watching the actors intently. He waved his arms at them now and then to modify a gesture, smiling happily at some farcical bit of pantomime.

We went into the Maeght villa together; he sat down next to me, not opposite me as I had expected. He had gone partly deaf in his left ear, he explained. This and a slowed-down gait were the only reminders that he was eighty-six years old.

As we talked, sounds of the Claca rehearsal could be heard through an open window. There was no formal plot to what they performed, but they improvised around the theme of an old Catalan folk tale, "The Death of the Monster." The Monster is the Tyrant, the Dictator, the anonymous embodiment of Evil.

Miró reminded me of his close attachment to the writing of Alfred Jarry since his first days in Paris; Jarry's fierce farce *Ubu Roi* epitomizes the grotesqueries of the modern condition. "I was swept off my feet by Jarry. And for my work with the Claca, my point of departure was Ubu——and obviously Ubu is a parallel with Franco. Jarry is more and

Program cover for *Ubu Roi*, by its author, Alfred Jarry.

Two Birds, 1977. Graphite on paper,
13 ⅝ x 11 ⅞ " (34.5 x 30 cm). Private
collection.

more relevant today. If my own *personnages* have become increasingly
grotesque, it is because we are living in a monstrous epoch. I am more
and more revolted by the world as it is. But I feel younger and keener
than ever, and more and more violent, and more and more free."

We talked about the exhibition. I told him how struck I was by the
intensity of the recent work, and by both the bite and the meticulousness
of the many drawings. "I draw a great deal these days," he said.

I told him how much I liked the backgrounds of the drawings—crumpled paper, sheets with random notations or lines of figures, spotted
cardboard, curious surfaces. "What the words or the figures mean is of
no interest to me. It is simply the form of the graphics I like. I draw on
anything. If I see a paper just left on the ground that says something to
me, I pick it up. Now, when I go back to Spain, there will be packages to
be opened. Often I'll keep the wrapping to use for drawings. I keep all
kinds of odd papers. Sometimes Pilar"—Miró's wife—"comes back from

Lithograph, late 1970s.

the market with food wrapped in paper with stains. I pounce on it for drawings. She is upset by this, but I can find a use for it. I also like beautiful Japanese papers."

I asked him about the role of the object for him at that time: "The form of an object for its own sake no longer seems to interest you as it once did. Perhaps it just serves to suggest something else?"

"Yes, that's it," he said. "A real object can prompt an idea for a painting or a sculpture. It might be the shock of a very small real object that starts me off. But more likely it will be something like this." He pointed to a space between the boards of the table in front of us. "Or if I see a shadow, or a crack in the wall, it can give me an idea. This line on the table, this black spot here, or that little mark there"—he touched them lovingly as he spoke, and a Miró seemed to come to life—"that releases the shutter . . . *pam!* I have to receive some kind of shock or I can't begin. Spots excite me. I am magnetized. It's like an electric current rushing through me."

I asked him how he began a canvas—did he use a drawing as a point of departure for a painting? "Sometimes I start with a drawing; I used to more often than now. Or it might be an accident of the canvas or paper. One or the other. An idea or automatism can be guided by the physicality of the material.

"Sometimes I start with brushes that are dirty: I wipe them across a new canvas"—he gestured back and forth. "I like old brushes, uneven, flattened out, that produce 'accidents.' If housepainters come to my place to do something, I say to them, 'Keep the oldest brushes you have. Don't throw them in the garbage can. Keep them for me.' An old brush has vitality"—he clacked his tongue appreciatively—"it's a brush that has lived, that has had a life of its own.

"I prefer objects that have lived. When I want to make a new painting, I buy a canvas at the art supplier's, but what is clean won't do. I begin to dirty it a bit, I splash it with turpentine, rub it with my paint-stained hands. I even walk on it. Or sometimes I use an old rag"—he made the gesture of rubbing paint onto a canvas with grouped fingers holding a rag—"or I begin with a piece of paper that I crumple up —*aaaaarrrhhh*— like this." An imaginary ball of paper was rubbed into an imaginary canvas.

"If the canvas is just new and clean, it's cold, it doesn't excite me."

Miró told me that more and more he wanted direct physical contact with his materials. "When I am making lithographs, I put my paws right into the ink. I used to work only with brushes, often very fine brushes,

People, Birds, 1977–78. Marble and glass mosaic, 28 x 52' (8.53 x 15.84 m). Edwin A. Ulrich Museum of Art, Wichita State University; Endowment Association Art Collection, Wichita, Kansas.

but now I need to get my hands into the paint or ink directly, to manipulate it. Sometimes I use my whole hand. Sometimes I dip all ten fingers into the paint and play with them on the canvas—like a pianist!" He gestured with all fingers.

In old age, this very small man was delighted with larger and larger projects. During our conversations that summer of 1979, Miró said that he hoped to come to America soon; he wanted to see his tapestry in the new wing of the National Gallery of Art in Washington, D.C. "Then of course," he said, "I want to go to *Vesheeta....*" It took me a few seconds to translate this to "Wichita."

"I made a big mosaic for Wichita, for the university. It's already installed, so I want to see the effect it makes. You know I have always talked to you about the importance to me of contact with people. That mosaic is on the exterior of one of the university buildings. And every

Poster for the 1979 Maeght Foundation exhibition, inscribed by Miró. Collection Rosamond Bernier, New York.

day, thousands of students go by that way. So, *évidemment*, it will have an effect on those boys, who are the men of tomorrow. One of them might be president of the United States. Seeing that mural might have an impact on him . . . so it's worthwhile. That's what interests me. It is the young people who count. I'm not interested in old dodos. I work for the

Miró and the author, 1979. Photo: Mrs.
Pierre Matisse.

future, for the year 2000. I work for the men of tomorrow—the men of today, *je m'en fous*."

We had been talking for a long time, and I worried that Miró might be getting tired. But he showed no sign of it. He beamed at me: "*Nous avons bien travaillé!*" But it was time to go to lunch. Before leaving, I asked him to sign the poster of the Maeght exhibition. I pulled off its protective wrapping; he uncurled the poster, looked at it intently, and selected a spot for his signature with great care. His pen hovered over the sheet and then came down like a dragonfly alighting. He considered his signature like a word floated on the canvas, part of the composition. . . . The accent on the *o* he described to me as an ascending form, a line of flight.

We walked together to the car. I realized I still had the crumpled wrapping paper in my hand, and looked around for a place to throw it away. Suddenly Miró said, "*Tu permets?*" and took the paper from me. He smoothed it out with eager anticipation, and with an apology took it into the house. In a moment, he came back, smiling.

"It's superb! I will take it back to Spain with me for a drawing. We have not only *bien travaillé ensemble*, we have collaborated!"

Photographic Credits

A NOTE ABOUT THE AUTHOR

Rosamond Bernier was the founding editor of *L'Œil*, an international art review published in Paris. She lectures regularly at the Metropolitan Museum of Art in New York, where her appearances are sold out six months in advance, and at many other museums in the United States. She has also recently been invited to lecture in the new auditorium in the Louvre in Paris. Thirteen of her lectures have been videotaped and televised throughout the United States by PBS.

In 1980 the French government made her an officer of the Order of Arts and Letters. In 1991 she was awarded an honorary doctorate in Humane Letters by Trinity College, Hartford, where she began her career as a lecturer in 1971.

Rosamond Bernier is also Editor-at-Large for cultural topics at *HG* and a Contributing Editor at *Vogue*. She lives in Connecticut with her husband, John Russell of *The New York Times*.

A NOTE ON THE TYPE

Pierre Simon Fournier (le jeune), who designed the types from which the typeface used in this book was adapted, was both an originator and a collector of types. His services to the art of printing were his design of letters, his creation of ornaments and initials, and his standardization of type sizes. His types are old style in character and sharply cut. In 1764 and 1768 he published his *Manuel Typographique*, a treatise on the history of French types and printing, on typefounding in all its details, and on what many consider his most important contribution to typography—the measurement of type by the point system.

Color separations by CCS, Clearwater, Florida
Printed and bound by R. R. Donnelley & Sons, Willard, Ohio
Designed by Peter A. Andersen